# Essential
# Budapest

## by

## CHRISTOPHER AND MELANIE RICE

Christopher Rice is a writer specialising in East European affairs. His wife, Melanie, is also a writer, and they have worked together on several children's books and guides.

Little, Brown and Co.
Boston        Toronto

The contents of this publication are believed correct at the time of printing. Nevertheless, the publishers cannot accept responsibility for errors or omissions, nor for changes in details given. We are always grateful to readers who let us know of any errors or omissions they come across, and future printings will be updated accordingly.

Produced by the Publishing Division of The Automobile Association of Great Britain.

Written by Christopher and Melanie Rice
"Peace and Quiet" section by Paul Sterry
Consultant: Frank Dawes

ISBN 0-316-25042-2

10 9 8 7 6 5 4 3 2 1

PRINTED IN TRENTO, ITALY

This book employs a
simple rating system to
help choose which
places to visit.

◆◆◆       do not miss

◆◆        see if you can

◆         worth seeing if
          you have time

## STREET NAMES

### STREET NAMES

Street names in Budapest are in the process of being changed and for some time the names printed on maps and those seen on the actual streets may not agree. The following list of old and new names (the most up-to-date available at the time of going to press) may help visitors to find their way around the city.

| Old | New |
|-----|-----|
| Antos István u. (XIV. ker.) | Bagolyvár u. |
| Asztalos János u. (I. ker.) | Aladár u. |
| Baktai Gyula u. (XIV. ker.) | Emilia u. |
| Beloiannisz u. (V. ker.) | Zoltán u. |
| Bihari Mor u. (III. ker.) | Apát u. |
| Bokányi Desző (VI. ker.) | Bajnok u. |
| Budafoki tér (XXII. ker.) | Szent István tér |
| Darvas József u. (III. ker.) | Szérűskert u. |
| Dimitrov tér (V. IX) | Fővám tér |
| Engels tér (V. ker.) | Erzsébet tér |
| Gajdán Imre u. (III. ker.) | Arvacska u. |
| Guszey u. (V. ker.) | Sas u. |
| Hámán Kató u. (IX. ker.) | Haller u. |
| Hatvany Lajos u. (I. ker.) | Kard u. |
| Hikádé Aladár u. (XIX. ker.) | Árpád u. |
| Ják köz (XXII. ker.) | Püspök u. |
| Károlyi Mihály u. egy része (V. ker.) | Ferenciek tere |
| Korvin Ottó tér (III. ker.) | Szentlélek tér |
| Korvin Ottó u. (III. ker.) | Pacsirtamező u. |
| Kruzslák Béla u. (XIII. ker.) | Gömb u. |
| Kun Béla rakpart (XIII. ker.) | Újpesti rakpart |
| László Jenő u (V. ker.) | Vajkay u. |
| Lengyel Gyula u. (V. ker.) | Bank u. |
| Lenin kőrút (VI. ker.) | Teréz kőrut |
| Lenin kőrút (VII. ker.) | Erzsébet kőrút |
| Lumumba u. (XIV. ker.) | Rona u. |
| Magyar Lajos u. (III. ker.) | Kis Korona u. |
| Majakovszkij u. (VI., VII. ker.) | Király u. |
| Május 1 út (XIV. ker) | Hermina út |
| Martos Flóra sétány (III. ker.) | Vasút sor |
| Mautner Sándor u. (XIII. ker.) | Szent László út |
| Merengo u. (XXII. ker.) | Kálváriahegy u. |
| Muck Lajos u. (XIII. ker.) | Thurzó u. |
| Münnich Ferenc u. (V. ker.) | Nádor u. |
| Nagytetényi Szolo ter (XXII. ker.) | Szentharomság tér |
| Néphadsereg tér (V. ker.) | Honvéd tér |
| Népköztársaság útja (VI. ker.) | Andrássy út |
| November 7. tér (VI. ker.) | Oktogon |
| Poscher János u. (XIII. ker.) | Kerekes u. |

| | |
|---|---|
| Rajk László u. (XIII. ker.) | Pannónia u. |
| Révai József u. (XIV. ker.) | Bácskai u. |
| Rosenberg házaspár u.. (V. ker.) | Hold u. |
| Rudas Laszló u. (VI. ker.) | Podmaniczky u. |
| Ságvári tér (V. ker.) | Vértanúk tere |
| Ságvári Endre u. (XVIII. ker.) | Gyöngyvirág u. |
| Sollner u. (XIII. ker.) | Násznagy u. |
| Somogyi Miklós u. (III. ker.) | Szent János u. |
| Szamuely u. (IX. ker.) | Lónyay u. |
| Szantó Béla u. (XIV. ker.) | Jávor u |
| Sziklai Sándor u. (I. ker.) | Lovas út |
| Tegzes u. (XXII. ker.) | Szent Korona u. |
| Thälmann u. (XIII. ker.) | Fiastyúk u. |
| Tisza Antal u. (XIII. ker.) | Tisza u. |
| Tolbuhin körút (V., IX. ker.) | Várnház körút |
| Vágó Béla u. (XIII. ker.) | Lomb u. |
| Vörös csillag u. (XIX. ker.) | Hofherr Albert u. |
| Vörös Hadsereg útja (III. ker.) | Királyok útja |
| Vörös Hadsereg útja (XVIII., XIX) | Üllöi út |
| Vörös október u. (XIX. ker.) | Vas Gereben u. |
| Zamercev tér (III. ker.) | Miklós u. |

*Times are changing for Hungary, but folk tradition remains strong*

## INTRODUCTION

Budapest, the capital of Hungary, lies at the very heart of Europe, Buda on the right, or west, bank of the famous River Danube (alas, no longer blue), Pest on the left, or east, bank. A busy, bustling city with more than two million inhabitants (one in every five Hungarians lives in Budapest), Buda and Pest together also make up the political, commercial and industrial hub of the entire country. Hungary, despite its small size (in area only two-thirds that of England), is at the cutting edge of the changes now transforming Central Europe. In April 1990 more than 40 parties contested the first free elections to be held since World War II. The overall winner was Jószef Antall's Democratic Forum – a centre-right grouping espousing capitalist values and a return to a more traditional sense of nationhood (the party's emblem shows the ancient coat of arms breaking through the grey mould of Soviet-imposed Communism). The biggest surprise, however, was the strong showing, especially in Budapest, of the new youth movement known as Fidesz. Predictably, this party has provided Hungary with its youngest MP – Tamás Deutsch, aged only 23.

*Recent events in Hungary have been momentous, but its history has ever been chequered: this 1849 print shows peasants in battle array during the War of Independence*

*Another significant period of Hungary's history was the 25-year regency of Miklós Horthy, seen here riding into Budapest at the head of his counter-revolutionary army in 1919*

Budapest has been centre-stage for a number of other remarkable events during the last few years, events full of symbolic significance for Hungarians: the reinterment of the disgraced former premier, Imre Nagy, the erection of a memorial to the victims of the holocaust, the removal of the red star from the Parliament Building, streets reverting to their pre-war names (November 7. tér to Oktogon for example). Budapest has also received a number of distinguished foreign guests recently – even the former heir to the imperial throne, Count Otto von Hapsburg, has visited the country in a symbolic act of reconciliation.

'Renewal' (the Hungarian equivalent of *Perestroika*) is currently transforming the face of commerce and industry. Trade barriers are coming down to facilitate closer ties with the EC countries – Hungary hopes eventually to become a member in its own right. State subsidies are being abolished and state industries sold off, collectivised farming is under review, private housing is now a reality (you can actually buy property through a real-estate agent in Budapest), the stock exchange has been revived, even credit cards are being

*Dressed in a highly decorative herdsman's costume, a zither player entertains tourists in the Fishermen's Bastion*

introduced. Most of these changes are welcomed by Hungarians but the side-effects are severe. Inflation, currently running at 30 per cent, is expected to rise further and unemployment too is on the increase. People are concerned about housing, the environment, rising crime and other problems. Yet, there is an overriding air of optimism, a confidence in the future.

Budapest is a beautiful city, as you will soon discover for yourself. It is also a fascinating one. There are the sights – Castle Hill, the Fishermen's Bastion, Parliament, Heroes' Square; the faded monuments of bygone eras; the splendid views across the Danube; the sidewalk cafés, restaurants and nightclubs; the excursions to the Buda Hills, the towns of the Danube Bend and Lake Balaton. You will find shops galore, tree-lined avenues, parks and museums – something for everyone in fact. That is the magic of Budapest. One word of warning, however. The language of the Hungarians (or Magyars, as they call themselves) is unlike any other most visitors will know and guesswork will get you nowhere with deciphering it.

## BACKGROUND

There were settlers in the area now made up by
Buda and Pest as long ago as 2000 BC and
probably much earlier (ornaments and graves
have been found on Csepel Island and on both
banks of the Danube). In the 6th century BC the
Scythians arrived from the northern shores of
the Black Sea, and in their wake came a number
of Celtic tribes from the area of modern France,
including the Eravisci, who inhabited the slopes
of Buda's Gellért Hill. The Eravisci were
craftsmen, familiar with the potter's wheel; some
of their work, coins and jewellery, for example,
has survived and may be seen in the Hungarian
National Museum.

*The view from the
roof-tops of Castle
Hill, Buda, across
the Danube to the
Parliament
building*

They were later assimilated by the Romans, who
had advanced their frontier to the Danube in the
1st century AD. The province of Pannonia (now
western Hungary) was divided in two in the
following century and Aquincum (now Óbuda)
became the capital. Aquincum was basically a
garrison town with 6,000–10,000 soldiers. An

amphitheatre was built for their entertainment and its remains can still be seen today near the Árpád Bridge. The Romans also built fortifications on the Pest side of the Danube and the bastion of the fortress known as Contra-Aquincum can be viewed in the centre of Március 15 tér.

**The Magyar Conquest**

When the imperial forces departed early in the 5th century, Aquincum was occupied for a time by the Huns (medieval chroniclers supposed that Buda was named after Attila's brother). Attila himself died in AD 453 and for several centuries thereafter Hungary was overrun by a succession of barbarian tribes. The Magyars followed the Avars, arriving in 896 from the Don-Volga region of what is now the Soviet Union, and immediately set out to conquer the entire Carpathian Basin. Their leader, Árpád, is said to have set up camp on Csepel Island, to the south of Budapest. Superb horsemen with a fearsome reputation, their restiveness soon led them to expand westwards in the direction of Bavaria and northern Italy until they were eventually halted in 933. Árpád's grandson, Prince Géza, embarked on a policy of consolidation which entailed the nation's conversion to Christianity (a decision taken purely for reasons of national security). His son, Stephen (István) won official recognition from the pope, who provided the crown for his coronation in December 1000. But Christianity was not imposed without a struggle: in 1046 Stephen's right-hand man, Bishop Gellért, was murdered by heathens on the hilltop which now bears his name.

As yet, Buda and Pest were insignificant villages. The centre of the kingdom was established, first at Esztergom and later at Székesfehérvár. However, during the 12th century French and German traders were officially encouraged to settle on the banks of the Danube and the future capital began gaining in importance.

**Medieval Budapest**

Disaster struck in 1241 when the Mongol Golden Horde crossed into Hungary and destroyed Pest. The terrified population fled to Buda but the following winter the Danube froze over and the

*Once Buda and Pest were villages on either side of the Danube. Elizabeth Bridge is one of several that connect them, forming the city of Budapest*

invaders installed themselves here as well. Things might have been even worse but for the sudden death of the supreme Khan, which led the warlord Batu Khan to return home in order to secure the succession. This unlooked-for breathing space allowed King Béla IV to emerge from hiding and set about improving the defences. Castles were built at various strategic points throughout the country, including Buda. At the same time, German settlers (soon to be joined by Magyar aristocrats) were invited to help repopulate the ravaged town.

The Árpád dynasty died in 1301 and a tussle for the succession ensued. The people of Buda favoured Wenceslas of Bohemia and when the pope expressed a preference for his rival,

Charles Robert of Anjou, they 'excommunicated' him in a ceremony held in the Church of Our Lady (now the Matthias Church). While the citizenry lost this particular contest – Charles Robert was eventually imposed on them – they gained when the Royal seat was moved to Buda from Visegrád. During the reigns of Louis (Lajos) I and the King-Emperor Sigismund of Luxembourg (1387–1437) the town flourished as never before. An imposing Gothic Palace rose up alongside the newly rebuilt Castle on the crown of Castle Hill. The ruins now form part of the Budapest History Museum. New religious foundations were erected, including the Dominican church and monastery whose remains have now been incorporated into the modern Hilton Hotel. The Hungarian population,

*Pest was destroyed in 1241 by Mongol hordes: it was Béla IV who refounded his nation. Below, modern Pest, seen from Buda*

which gravitated towards the north end of Castle Hill near the Magdalen Tower, was effaced by foreign communities of merchants and artisans – French in Fortuna utca, Italians in Országház utca and Germans in the neighbourhood of the Matthias Church. The Jews, too, were here and had their own Prayer House and cemetery.

### The Turkish Occupation

Buda reached its apogee in the reign of Matthias (Mátyás) Corvinus (1458–90) when the court became a centre of Renaissance learning, boasting one of the largest libraries in Europe. Artists and craftsmen from Italy were invited by the king and his second wife, Beatrice of Aragon (a friend of Lorenzo de Medici) to work on the refurbishment of the royal palace.

With Matthias' death, Hungary fell into irreversible decline. His successor, Wladislaw of Bohemia, was weak and vacillating and the nobility took full advantage, arrogantly usurping his authority and pursuing their territorial claims with a suicidal singlemindedness. Oppressed beyond endurance, the impoverished peasants staged a rebellion which was mercilessly suppressed (their leader, György Dózsa, was roasted alive). The divided loyalties inspired by the Reformation reduced the kingdom to anarchy, making it ripe for conquest. In 1526 the Turks, who had been threatening to attack for some time, defeated the Hungarian forces at Mohács. Buda fell in 1541, initiating an occupation that was to last for 150 years.

The Turks have generally had a bad press, but of course their own chroniclers saw things differently. There are some splendid Turkish baths surviving in Budapest but otherwise little of their contribution remains today. They improved the fortifications around the castle but allowed the royal palace and many of the merchant houses to fall into ruin. Most of the churches were turned into mosques.

After sustaining a dozen sieges, Buda was finally recaptured by a joint European force in 1686. Pope Innocent XI, who financed the venture, is given much of the credit and his statue now stands in the centre of Hess András tér.

### Hapsburg Budapest

Having shaken off one foreign power, the Hungarians now found themselves dominated by another. The Austrian Hapsburgs ruled from Vienna and discouraged independent activity, though they did allow limited progress in the commercial and industrial spheres. Their major contribution, however, was an architectural one. Buda was rebuilt in the baroque and neo-classical styles then fashionable and inhabited by wealthy Hungarian merchants and princes. But beneath the veneer of wealth and contentment was a growing Hungarian nationalism. From time to time, this erupted into open rebellion. The armed struggle, led by Prince Ferenc Rákóczi II from 1703 to 1711, was eventually defeated, as was the Jacobin conspiracy of 1795, which resulted in the

*Sedilia such as these in the Castle district have been preserved from Buda's medieval days*

beheading of Ignác Martinovics and his fellow conspirators in what is still known as 'blood meadow' (Vérmező).

In the face of overwhelming odds, violent confrontation was almost bound to end in failure. Acknowledging this painfully acquired lesson, the Reform Movement of the early 19th century sought to pursue similar goals by peaceful means. Its most influential exponent was Count István Széchenyi (1791–1860), a firm believer in material and scientific progress. England was his model: 'England has learned three things that we must learn,' he told his fellow countrymen after returning from one of many visits abroad, 'the constitution, engineering and horse-breeding.' Constitutional reform had to wait but horse-racing was introduced in 1827. For the first time too, Buda, not Pest, became the main focus of economic and social activity. Hungary's first university had already been transferred here in 1784. In 1802 Ferenc Széchenyi (István's father) conceived the idea of

*While much of
Buda's charm dates,
as above, from the
18th century, it
was the 19th
century that saw
Pest's architectural
flowering*

a National Museum, a project finally realised in
1848. An Academy of Sciences was founded in
1830 and a National Theatre seven years later.
Széchenyi himself will always be associated
with the Chain Bridge which bears his name, the
first permanent link between Buda and Pest,
completed under British supervision in 1849.
The era of peaceful reform was destined not to
last. In March 1848, following news of rioting in
Vienna, crowds began to gather in the centre of
Pest. They were addressed from the steps of the
National Museum by the self-appointed leaders
of the revolution, among them the young poet,
Sándor Petőfi, whose famous 'Song' was
rapturously received. A newly formed
provisional government under Count Lajos
Batthyány declared Hungary independent.
Backs to the wall, the Austrians made
concessions, but early in 1849 the battle was

rejoined. At first the Hungarian forces had the upper hand but Russia's intervention on the side of Austria proved decisive. Retribution was swift. Batthyány and 13 rebel generals were executed. Others suffered torture, imprisonment or exile. The fortress known as the Citadella, which still dominates the approaches to Gellért Hill, stands as a reminder of the Austrian presence at its most oppressive. In 1867, however, changing circumstances resulted in a change of policy: the *Ausgleich*, or Compromise, granted a measure of autonomy to Hungary within the framework of a Dual Monarchy and ushered in a period of spectacular capitalist development.

### *Fin de Siècle* Budapest

Within 30 years, Budapest (the two towns were amalgamated in 1873) had become one of the leading cities of Europe. The sidewalk cafés lining new thoroughfares like Andrássy Avenue and the Great Boulevard became the haunt of a self-confident intellectual élite. Tourists from all over Europe patronised the grand hotels jostling for pre-eminence along the Corso. Migrant workers from the rural hinterland left the slums of the outer city for the giant concerns of Hungary's industrial revolution, Weiss, Ganz and Óbuda Shipbuilding. New bridges spanned the Danube, modern municipal services were introduced, the first underground railway system on the European mainland was constructed and an unprecedented building boom turned the city into a showpiece of architectural eclecticism.

In 1896 the millenary celebrations, marking the thousandth anniversary of the Magyar conquest, took place in Budapest. Thousands of visitors, in holiday mood, came to the City Park to inspect the stands and exhibition tents and to marvel at Alpár's Vajdahunyad Castle. There was an overwhelming atmosphere of self-congratulation in the air, a confidence in Hungary's future, symbolised in that quintessential architectural monument, the Parliament building.

### War, Revolution and Independence

World War I shattered these illusions of permanence and prosperity. Shackled to Austria and consequently bound by her alliance with

*Shortly after its completion, the Art Nouveau Hotel Gellért was taken over by Horthy as his headquarters*

Germany, Hungary found herself on the side of the defeated. Amid the ruins of the former Empire, independence was proclaimed and a republic adopted; Mihály Károlyi became the first president in January 1919. But the hold of the new regime was precarious, especially in Budapest where prisoners of war returning from internment in Russia fuelled the discontent of a starving and disease-ridden population. The Communists seized power and created a Soviet-style workers' republic under Béla Kun. This in turn collapsed after 133 days when the nationalist, Admiral Miklós Horthy led an army of 25,000 into Budapest and established his headquarters in the Gellért Hotel.

Horthy's authoritarian rule and his determination to regain the territories lost in the post-war settlement, made him a natural ally of the Nazis and in 1941 Hungary entered World War II on

*Chapel of Ják, Vajdahunyad Castle, in City Park. The castle was built for the millenary exhibition of 1896*

the side of Germany. However, growing doubts about Horthy's reliability led to the occupation of Budapest in March 1944. The inevitable persecution of Jews, Communists and other anti-Fascists was followed in the autumn by a reign of terror masterminded by the Hungarian Arrow Cross. Thousands of Jews were deported but thanks to the intervention of the young Swedish attaché, Raoul Wallenberg, some at least avoided the death camps. Wallenberg himself disappeared in the chaos of the final months of the war. By the time the Soviets took control in February 1945, the city was in ruins.

### People's Republic

In the post-war years, Communist rule was consolidated under Stalin's henchman, Mátyás Rákosi and the country was collectivised and industrialised on the Soviet model. A

## BACKGROUND

*A decorative reminder of Buda's more grandiose days*

reconstructed Budapest rose from the ashes but life in the capital remained grim. Show trials, political repression and economic hardship were the main ingredients in the explosive mix which detonated the Hungarian Uprising of October 1956. All the principal events took place in Budapest – the march of 50,000 protestors from Bem József tér to Parliament, the siege of the radio building, the beheading of Stalin's statue near the City Park and the fighting itself. The tanks rolled in on 4 November. The impact of the uprising was huge, and change was inevitable. The new leader, János Kádár, gradually brought about a transition from political totalitarianism to a consensus between leadership and people. His 32-year rule finally ended when he was ousted from power in 1988.

### A New Start

Today Budapest is a happier place as the people contentedly throw off the shackles of Soviet occupation, removing the red stars from the Parliament building and from the park on Gellért Hill, renaming the streets, rehabilitating formerly disgraced politicians like Imre Nagy – all in a heady atmosphere of democratic renewal and economic entrepreneurship. As Hungary's new government bids to become a member of the European Community, Budapest faces west, hopefully towards a brighter future.

## WHAT TO SEE

The places of interest described here are listed alphabetically in three sections – Buda, Pest, and Around Budapest.

Included are some of the 80 or more museums and galleries in Budapest, catering to the specialist and general visitor alike. Opening times are the latest available, but it is a good idea to check at the information desk of your hotel before setting out. Subjects range from stamp collecting to pharmacy, from fine arts to transportation. As in most countries of Eastern Europe, the displays are often unimaginatively presented, but the most serious drawback is the absence of catalogues and information in English (or in most other European languages). Hopefully, the recent social and political changes in Hungary will lead to improvements here as well.

For special exhibitions, see the monthly brochure *Programme in Hungary* available at Tourist Information Centres.

### Buda

The delights of historical Buda make it the first port of call of every tourist. You will want to begin with a view from Pest across the Danube and there are two ideal vantage points. Probably the better (and slightly less spoiled by the constant roar of traffic) is from Széchenyi rakpart in front of the Orsághaz (Parliament building). From here you will easily be able to pick out the spire of the Mátyás-templom (Matthias Church) on top of Várhegy (Castle Hill) and the outline of the Víziváros (Watertown) district below. From nearby Kóssuth Lajos tér you can take Metro line 2 across

*Buda, with Matthias Church and Fishermen's Bastion, seen from Pest*

the river to Batthyány tér, then walk along Fő utca and climb one of the narrow streets up to Halászbástya (Fishermen's Bastion).

Alternatively, you can cross by the Széchenyi lánchíd (Chain Bridge), the other excellent viewing point, and pick up the funicular railway (Budavári Sikló) from Clark Ádám tér. (Buy your ticket at the turnstile.) On a hot day this saves a tiring climb, but you may have to wait in line. Good for views and photographs of Pest as you go up.

A third approach is to take the No. 16 bus from Erzsébet tér (Engels tér), which winds its way up Castle Hill to Dísz tér (also handy for the Royal Palace and museums).

◆
### ARANY SAS PATIKAMÚZEUM (ARANY SAS (GOLDEN EAGLE) PHARMACY MUSEUM)

*Tárnok utca 18*
All the tools of the pharmaceutical trade, dating back to the late Middle Ages, are exhibited here. The house itself is 15th-century and there has been a pharmacy on the premises for more than 200 years.
*Open:* Tuesday to Sunday 10:30A.M.–5:30P.M.
*Closed:* Monday

◆◆
### BUDAPESTI TÖRTÉNETI MÚZEUM (BUDAPEST HISTORY MUSEUM/CASTLE MUSEUM)

*Royal Palace, Castle Hill*
Occupying the southern end of the former Palace, Wing E, the museum is divided into two sections. The remains of the medieval palace, together with

## WHAT TO SEE

sculptures, ceramics, pots and pans, and weapons can be seen on the lower floor, a maze of labyrinthine passageways, cellars and vaulted halls. Above is an exhibition devoted to the 2,000-year history of Budapest, containing the usual array of photographs, prints and posters and, more unusually, survivals from the Turkish occupation. Unfortunately, there is no English language commentary.

**Magyar Munkásmozgalmi Múzeum (The Museum of the Hungarian Workers' Movement)**, situated in the opposite, northern wing of the palace (Wing A), may be of interest to those studying labour history. A ponderous celebration of Communism's supposed triumphs (in Hungary and outside) the exhibition is rapidly becoming an embarrassment to the authorities and its days, in its present form, are numbered. (Some kind of amalgamation with the Hungarian National Museum is planned.)
*Open:* Tuesday to Sunday 10:00A.M–6:00P.M.
*Closed:* Monday

*Gellért monument, Gellért Hill*

## GELLÉRT-HEGY (GELLÉRT HILL)

The best vantage point from which to see Budapest, Gellért Hill looms over the Castle District, rising to a height of 430 feet (130m) between the Erzsébet (Elizabeth) and Szabadság (Freedom) Bridges. Vines used to grow on these rugged slopes but a phylloxera epidemic mid-way through the last century killed off the entire crop. There are numerous points of access; the most direct approach is to take any one of the footpaths which wind their way around the hill in the vicinity of Elizabeth Bridge. Alternatively, the No. 27 bus will take you to the top from Móricz Zsigmond körtér. If you have a car, you can take one of the side roads around Szirtes út, which leads directly to the Citadella (taxis are available at both these points). The hill is named after Bishop Gellért (Gerard), who was summoned from Italy by King Stephen to help convert the Magyars to Christianity. A massive statue of the saint, framed by a semi-circular colonnade, overlooks the Elizabeth Bridge from the spot where, it is said, a group of obdurate heathens cast him off in a barrel during a rebellion several years after the king's death. Defiant to the last, the grim-faced bronze figure raises a cross high above the city. An artificial waterfall runs below. At the bottom of the hill, on the Szent Gellért rakpart, are the **Rudas Baths**, part of which date from the time of the Turkish occupation. Built by Pasha

Mustapha in 1566, an octagonal pool has a magnificent domed roof.

**The Citadella**, on the crown of the hill, is a fortress of white stone constructed by the Austrians to quell the population in the aftermath of the 1848–9 War of Independence. Gaps were later made in the walls to symbolise the restoration of good relations following the Compromise of 1867. Today there is nothing more intimidating than the prices in the restaurant.

**Felszabadulás emlékmű (Liberation Monument)**, beside the Citadella, overlooking the river, was built to commemorate the Soviet-led liberation of Budapest from the Nazis in 1945. The designer was a Hungarian, Zsigmond Kisfaludi-Strobl, but the inscription on the base is in Russian and reads: 'To the liberating Soviet heroes from a grateful Hungarian people.' The statue of the Socialist-realist heroine, holding a palm in both hands, is one of the city's landmarks, a role which will probably save it from the fate of the metal red star which was removed recently from the nearby park. Away from the monument in the direction of the Freedom Bridge, is Szent Gellért tér, where the famous **Hotel Gellért** and the **Gellért Baths** are situated. The hotel, in Art Nouveau style, was once the headquarters of the Hungarian dictator, Admiral Horthy. On the slopes of Gellért Hill you can see the houses and apartments of some of the well-heeled inhabitants of present-day Budapest.

## WHAT TO SEE

### HADTÖRTENÉTI MÚZEUM (MILITARY HISTORY MUSEUM)
*Kapisztrán tér*
A former barracks, the museum contains exhibits relating to the 1848–9 War of Independence and beyond.
*Open:* Tuesday to Saturday 9:00A.M.–5:00P.M., Sunday 10:00A.M.–6:00P.M.
*Closed:* Monday

### ◆◆◆
### HALÁSZBÁSTYA (FISHERMEN'S BASTION)
*Castle Hill*
On the eastern edge of Castle Hill, near the Mátyás-templom (Matthias Church), this entertaining architectural fantasy was built at the end of the 19th century to coincide with the city's 1,000th anniversary celebrations. The designer was Frigyes Schulek, who obviously enjoyed letting his imagination run riot after toiling away at church restoration. It gets its name from the fishermen of the Víziváros (Watertown) district who traditionally defended this section of the fortifications. The seven tent-shaped turrets represent the seven Hungarian tribes who made their home here. Walk along the parapets to get a superb view of the city and river (smog permitting). No marks for spotting the Parliament building and the unmistakable dome of St Stephen's Church. Lined up along the embankment, which used to be called the Corso, you should also be able to make out three of Pest's premier hotels: the Atrium Hyatt, the Forum and the Intercontinental. The Széchenyi lánchíd (Chain Bridge) spans the river near by. On your left, in the distance, is the tree-shrouded Margit-sziget (Margaret Island). The arches and recesses of the Bastion provide welcome shade from the hot summer sun and an opportunity to rest the legs. It is also a good place to write those postcards home. The stalls selling lace and other crafted articles have tourists in mind and the prices may therefore be on the steep side. On the other hand, buy a few presents here now and it may save you a lot of foot-slogging later.

### ◆

### MAGYAR KERESKEDELMI ÉS VENDÉGLÁTÓIPARI MÚZEUM (HUNGARIAN COMMERCE AND CATERING MUSEUM)
*Fortuna utca 4*
Occupying the premises of an 18th-century inn, this relatively new museum traces the history of the retailing of Hungarian food and drink. Recorded commentary in English available.
*Open:* Tuesday to Sunday 10:00A.M.–6:00P.M.
*Closed:* Monday

### ◆◆

### MAGYAR NEMZETI GALÉRIA (HUNGARIAN NATIONAL GALLERY)
*Royal Palace, Castle Hill*
Four floors of the former Royal Palace are devoted to all aspects of Hungarian art and sculpture from medieval times to the present day. The collection includes altarpieces, wood panels and paintings dating from the 15th and 16th centuries; work by the important 19th-century

artist Mihály Munkácsy (once renowned throughout Europe and honoured with a hero's funeral in Budapest), Pál Szinyei Merse, and László Paál; and some interesting 20th-century paintings showing the influence of the Western Cubist and Expressionist schools on Béla Czóbel, Lajos Tihanyi and Lajos Kassák, among others.

*Open:* Tuesday to Sunday 10:00 A.M.–6:00 P.M.
*Closed:* Monday

**Fishermen's Bastion**

## WHAT TO SEE

### ◆◆◆
### MÁTYÁS-TEMPLOM (MATTHIAS CHURCH)

*Szentháromság tér (Trinity Square)*

Founded by King Béla IV in about 1250, the church—actually dedicated to the Virgin Mary—takes its name from Mátyás (Matthias) Corvinus, who added the finishing touches in the second half of the 15th century. The Turks turned it into a mosque, removing the furnishings and white-washing the walls. Two chandeliers from the high altar can still be seen in Saint Sophia's in Constantinople. The Jesuits celebrated the reconsecration of the church by fitting it out in sumptuous baroque style. They also built a college next door, where the Hilton Hotel now stands. By the 19th century, urgent repairs were needed to the church's exterior. One of Hungary's most distinguished architects, Frigyes Schulek, undertook the restoration, which was completed in 1896. Very little of the original building now remains. The church has been the setting for many famous historical events. It was here in 1302 that the citizens of Buda 'excommunicated' Pope Boniface VIII for daring to support Charles Robert of Anjou's claim to the throne over that of their own candidate, Wenceslas of Bohemia. Matthias Corvinus married Beatrice of Aragon here in the 15th century, and it was here also that the last Hapsburg rulers, Franz Josef I and Charles IV were crowned, in 1867 and 1916 respectively. Enter the church through the Mary Portal where you can still see a 14th-century relief depicting the death of the Virgin. The main body of the church is 19th-century but the dazzling interior decoration with its painted floral motifs is based on the original medieval designs. The church has strong musical associations. Liszt's *Coronation Mass* and Kodály's *Te Deum* were both first performed here and the tradition continues with regular concerts and recitals (Friday evenings in the summer, tickets available at the door). On Sundays there is a sung high mass at 10:00A.M., sometimes with orchestral accompaniment. In the Loreto Chapel, to the left of the Mary Portal as you go in, there is a Gothic triptych and a baroque black madonna dating from about 1700. Note the original coat of arms of Matthias Corvinus (The Raven) on the wall by the main altar. The chapel nearest the main door on the opposite side of the church is dedicated to St Imre, son of the first Christian king of Hungary, St Stephen. Next to it is the Holy Trinity chapel, where you will find the tomb of the 12th-century king, Béla III, and his wife, Anne of Chatillon, although their remains were moved here only in 1848.

The two oratories, the chapel of St Stephen and the crypt (access to the side of the main pulpit) all contain exhibits from the Museum of Ecclesiastical Art. To the side of the church is a large equestrian statue of St Stephen (note the cross and halo).

*Matthias Church*

## WHAT TO SEE

### ◆◆◆
### VÁRHEGY (CASTLE) HILL

*You need special permission to take a private car on to Castle Hill.*

You can easily spend a day in the Castle district. It is probably best to visit the more picturesque streets (see below) in the morning, before the crowds arrive, and leave the Royal Palace and museums for the afternoon.

Buda and Pest were distinct communities until they were joined, by administrative fiat, in 1873 and they are still vastly different in appearance. Buda stretches rather lazily along the slopes of Castle Hill, a mile-long plateau of craggy limestone overlooking the Danube from a height of 200 feet (60m). Its history has been troubled and turbulent. The first settlement here was destroyed by the Mongols in 1241, inducing Béla IV, somewhat belatedly, to improve the defences. He built a castle and the citizens made new homes for themselves around the royal quarters. A thriving community developed and, by the beginning of the 16th century, Buda was known throughout Europe as a centre of Renaissance learning. Dark times were about to return, however. The Turks were already knocking at the gates and in 1541 they seized the castle, beginning an occupation which was to last almost 150 years. Buda then fell into decline. The Royal Palace was abandoned and most of the inhabitants fled, the churches were despoiled and turned into mosques. On the positive side, the invaders improved the fortifications and built the bath houses which are still a tourist attraction today. The Turks were finally expelled in 1686 but recovery was slow and Buda never really regained its old importance. Its charm today stems from a decision of the new Austrian rulers to rebuild from scratch in the baroque style, and the uniform elegance which resulted makes its streets a delight to stroll in. It is hard to believe that all this is the product of painstaking restoration work following the town's almost total destruction at the end of World War II.

**Út, utca (streets) and tér (squares) of the Castle District**
**Dísz tér**, once known as Pasha Square (a reminder of the Turkish occupation), was formerly a parade ground. The statue of the soldier commemorates the heroes of the War of Independence of 1848–9. **Tárnok utca** is one of the most attractive streets in Buda. As with most of the streets here, the houses are largely of 18th-century design, built on medieval foundations and still retaining fragments of the earlier features. The word *tárnok* means treasurer and the street was once the hub of Buda's commercial life. The building with the rusty patterning at No. 14 dates from the 14th and 15th centuries (the protruding first floor was the medieval hall). Adjoining it is the wine bar and restaurant called the Arany Hordó (Golden Barrel). No. 18 is the **Arany Sas Patikamúzeum (Golden Eagle Pharmacy Museum)** (see entry above). The original building dates from the 15th century. There is a post office in Tárnok utca (note the old red mailbox outside). **Szentháromság tér** (Trinity

*Táncsics Mihály, one of Castle Hill's picturesque streets*

Square) is named after the monument to the Holy Trinity in the centre. It was erected by the grateful survivors of a plague in the 18th century. The building at No. 7 is the famous **Ruszwurm pastry shop**, which has been producing mouth-watering aromas since it opened in 1827. The two-storey baroque building on the corner of Szentháromság utca is the old Buda Town Hall. You will also be able to see Halászbástya (the Fishermen's Bastion) and part of the Hilton Hotel. But the dominant feature of the square is undoubtedly the **Mátyás-templom (Matthias**

*The Post Office in Tárnok utca, with its old red mailbox*

**Church)** (see separate entry). **Hess András tér** passes in front of the Hilton Hotel. The hotel was built in 1976 on the site of a Dominican church and monastery. In keeping with modern architectural fashion, the ruins have been incorporated into the overall design. The main front of the hotel also bears traces of the 18th-century Jesuit college which used to stand here. Not everyone appreciates this peculiar mix of old and new, but the Hilton, which has recently been spruced up, is the focus of Buda nightlife and so cannot be ignored. Charming Hess András tér gets its name from Hungary's first printer, who had a shop here in the 15th

century. The statue in the middle is of Pope Innocent XI who inspired the Christians to defeat and finally expel the Turks in the 1680s. The 18th-century building to the rear of the statue is a former inn called the Red Hedgehog (you can see its delightful emblem over the main door). There were originally three medieval houses on the site and you can still see traces of them in the main door and window frames. There is now an antiques shop here.

**Táncsics Mihály utca**, is named after one of the heroes of the 1848 uprising. The elegant building at No. 7 was once an 18th-century palace and is now the **Zenetörténeti Múzeum**

**(Music History Museum)** (see entry below). Even if you don't want to visit the museum, at least have a look at the splendid baroque courtyard. Beethoven stayed here when he visited Buda to give a series of concerts in 1800. Another musical genius, the Hungarian composer Béla Bartók, later set up a workshop here and the museum displays some of his autographed scores. No. 9 has at various times served as royal mint, barracks and prison. During the War of Independence with the Austrians, many leading revolutionaries, including Táncsics and his more famous comrade-in-arms, Lajos Kossuth, were incarcerated in the dungeons here. The yellow building at No. 16 has an attractive 18th-century mural between the windows on the first floor. No. 26 reminds us that this was once the Jewish quarter of the town. There are ancient tombstones on display in this house which once served as a synagogue. At the end of the street is the Bécsi kapu or Vienna Gate, a reconstruction built in 1936 to mark the 250th anniversary of the expulsion of the Turks from Buda. The German novelist, Thomas Mann, lived in the square, at No. 7, from 1935 to 1936.

**Fortuna utca** is named after an 18th-century inn which used to be situated at No. 4. The building is now occupied by the **Magyar Kereskedelmi és Vendéglátóipari Múzeum (Hungarian Museum of Commerce and Catering)** (see separate entry).

**Orságház utca**, or Parliament

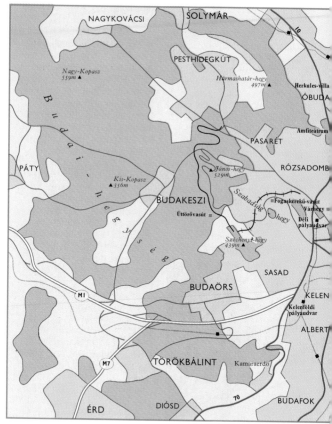

Street, is a reminder of the days when Buda was much more than an oversized, if picturesque, museum. During the 1790s both Houses of the Hungarian Diet, or Parliament, met at No. 28, so conditions must have been fairly cramped. No. 2, now a restaurant, occupies the site of a 15th-century mansion. The cloister-like courtyard contains many clues to its medieval past, such as the sedilia (stone seats)

in the doorway and the surviving stone arches. The houses at Nos. 18, 20 and 22 are also medieval in origin, although all have been heavily reconstructed.

**Kapisztrán tér** is at the far end of the street, dominated by the 13th-century Magdalen tower, sadly all that now remains of the church of that name. The yellow building at No. 40 is the **Hadtörténeti Múzeum (Museum of Military History)** (see entry).

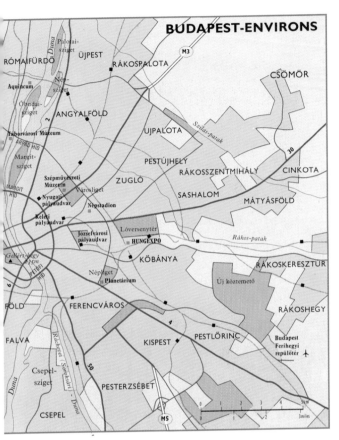

BUDAPEST-ENVIRONS

**Úri utca**'s courtyards (particularly Nos. 31, 32, 34, 36, 38 and 40) contain more medieval remnants, No. 31 being the best preserved of all. A visit to the **Budavári Panoptikum (Buda Castle Wax Works)**, situated at No. 9, is the only way nowadays to see what remains of the underground passageways and caves that used to criss-cross beneath the town. Turks and Christians alike made good use of them as a means of deploying troops and surprising enemies. Later, they were converted into cellars which made ideal air-raid shelters during World War II. Now a waxworks depicts scenes from Magyar history. *Open:* Tuesday to Sunday 10:00A.M.–6:00P.M.

**Tóth Árpád sétány**, the western ramparts of the Castle District, offer a good view of the Buda hills.

## WHAT TO SEE

### ◆◆
### VÁRPALOTA (THE ROYAL PALACE)

*Castle Hill*

The Royal Palace, razed to the ground and rebuilt countless times, suffered some degree of destruction and reconstruction with every twist and turn of Buda's equally turbulent history. It was originally built in the second half of the 13th century by Béla IV after the invasion of the Mongols. The Angevin kings later enlarged it; the recently discovered foundations of the István tower, plus the reconstructed crypt of the Royal chapel, are relics of those times. Under the Holy Roman Emperor Sigismund of Luxembourg (king of Hungary from the late 14th century to the mid-15th century) the palace was enlarged again, this time in the Gothic style. Today sections from this time, such as the vast Knights Hall, have been reconstructed. When King Matthias (Mátyás) (1458–90) came to the throne, then began what is generally regarded as the golden age of the Palace (and of Buda generally). Most of the castle was rebuilt in the Italian Renaissance style and new buildings were added; many politicians, artists and scholars visited the Palace as it became

*The Music History Museum, where Béla Bartók had his workshop*

known as a centre of European culture (and a place where the hospitality was lavish). When the Turks invaded they did little damage to the great Renaissance edifice but it was finally and tragically destroyed during the great siege of 1686. The Austrian Hapsburgs became Hungary's new rulers in the early 18th century and they levelled the ruins of the former magnificent edifice and began work on a smaller palace of their own. In 1800 Joseph Haydn conducted his oratorio *The Creation* in the ceremonial hall of the new palace. Throughout the 19th century the palace was expanded and renovated (one of the wings and the middle of the palace was destroyed by fire in 1849). The neo-baroque form that the building took on was the work of the architect Miklós Ybl (he added the building which today houses the National Széchényi Library). Alajos Hauszmann took over as architect when Ybl died and completed the construction of the symmetrical palace building in 1905.

The troubles were not over though; in World War II the palace was completely burnt out. Work began on reconstruction in the 1950s – it was only completed during the 1980s. Remains of the original, medieval palace were found and can be seen by visitors today. The renovated Palace was built with modern interiors to house cultural and state institutions; several major museums can be seen within its confines, including the **Magyar Nemzeti Galéria (Hungarian National Gallery)**, the **Budapesti Történeti Múzeum (Budapest History Museum/ Castle Museum)** and the **Magyar Munkásmozgalmi Múzeum (Museum of the Hungarian Workers' Movement)** (see separate entries).

Leaving via the northern end of the Palace complex, note the impressive yellow building marked **Várszínház** between Szent György tér and adjoining Dísz tér. This is the **Castle Theatre**. Originally a church, it was redesigned in the 1780s. Shortly afterwards, the first Hungarian theatre company began performing here. The relief just inside the entrance commemorates a concert given by Beethoven in 1800.

◆
## ZENETÖRTÉNETI MÚZEUM (MUSIC HISTORY MUSEUM)
*Táncsics Mihály utca 7*
As the entrance to this imposing building suggests, it once belonged to a Hungarian nobleman. Beethoven lived here for a while in 1800, and the 20th-century Hungarian composer, Béla Bartók, set up a workshop on the premises. On display are a motley collection of old instruments manufactured in Hungary (including some splendid examples of folk instruments) as well as a special exhibition on the life and work of Bartók. All this would be fascinating if only there was a translation. A charming old man called János does his best to help out!
*Open:* Monday 4:00–9:00 P.M.; Wednesday to Sunday 10:00 A.M.–6:00 P.M.
*Closed:* Tuesday

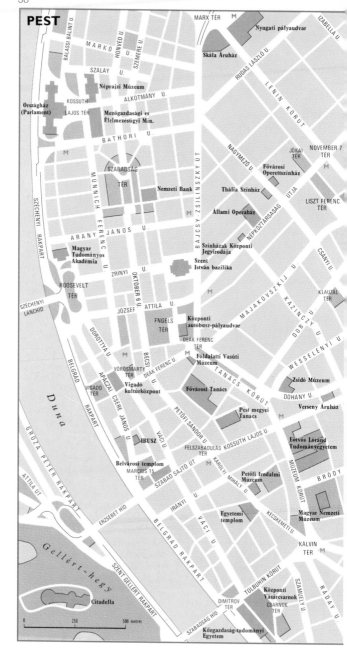

**PEST**

## Pest

While there have been settlers
on the left bank of the Danube
since ancient times, the present
appearance of Pest (pronounced
*pesht* by Hungarians) owes most
to the period from 1840 onwards
when the city became the focus
of a cultural renewal inspired by
anti-Austrian resistance.
Following the Compromise of
1867, Pest was transformed,
along with Buda, into an imperial
capital equal in status with
Vienna. But virtually all the
subsequent construction boom
was concentrated on the left
bank and the Art Nouveau and
Eclectic styles then fashionable
have left their indelible mark on
the city. The great stone
embankment known as the
Corso, already a favourite with
promenaders, was now lined
with a series of grandiose hotels,
each more opulent than the last.
Today only the names have
changed. Hungary's enhanced
political status was encapsulated
in the huge Parliament building
(then the largest in the world)
which rose up near by.
Government, banking and
insurance offices and the largest
stock exchange in Europe
added to Pest's growing sense
of self-importance. New bridges
were built across the Danube
and the first underground
railway on the European
mainland was built beneath
Andrássy Avenue
(Népköztársaság útja). This
resplendent thoroughfare, like
so much in Pest reminiscent of
Wilhelminian Berlin, became the
linchpin of a new network of
boulevards and beltways which
still exists, although the names

have undergone various changes.

Pest is inextricably linked to the more dramatic moments in Hungary's modern history. The poet Petőfi proclaimed the country's independence from the steps of the National Museum in 1848. Béla Kun established a short-lived Soviet republic here in 1919. A quarter of a century later, German and Soviet troops were fighting over every square yard of the city (you can still see the bullet holes in the Jewish district). And the former radio building and secret police headquarters are reminders of the ill-starred Hungarian revolution of 1956. Today, Pest is a city to stroll and browse in – don't make the mistake of trying

*The sumptuous State Opera House*

to cover too much ground at once. If you get tired of sightseeing, there's always the restful Városliget (City Park) or any of the numerous cafés and bars which line the main avenues. And Pest's modern shopping streets, with their eye-catching displays, make it a home-away-from-home for Westerners.

◆◆◆
## ALLAMI OPERAHÁZ (STATE OPERA HOUSE)
*Andrássy út (Népköztársaság útja)*
One of the most important buildings in the history of Hungarian architecture, the State Opera House in Budapest also ranks among the most beautiful in Europe; its interior possibly the richest in the city.

The Emperor Franz Josef commissioned Miklós Ybl to design an opera house for Budapest to compete with the finest in Europe; he certainly achieved this and in doing so produced what is considered by many to be his *opus magnum*. Construction began in 1875; marbled, gilded and decorated with frescos by some of the finest painters of the time, this elegant neo-Renaissance building opened nine years later in 1884. Standards were high from the first: Gustav Mahler was Music Director for a time and, after World War II, so was Otto Klemperer. Its last great director was János Ferencsik who died in 1984.

The balconied façade of the building is adorned with statues of the great composers: Monteverdi, Scarlatti, Gluck, Mozart, Beethoven, Rossini, Donizetti, Glinka, Wagner, Verdi, Gounod, Bizet, Mussorgsky, Tchaikovsky, Moniusko and Smetana. First-floor niches hold Terpsichore, Erato, Thalia and Melpomene, to represent dance, love-poetry, comedy and tragedy.

Inside the vast auditorium, seating an audience of around 1,300 and facing a stage 47 yards (43m) deep, a three-ton, bronze chandelier hangs from a ceiling decorated with a fine fresco by Károly Lotz; it shows Greek Gods with Apollo, the God of Music in the centre. . Other paintings in the public rooms include those by Mór Than and Bertalan Székely.

While Budapest's opera house was under construction, a particularly tragic fire destroyed the Ringtheatre in Vienna, killing over 400 people. As a result, all-metal, hydraulic stage machinery, an iron curtain and sprinkler system were installed in Budapest's new opera house. It was the most modern theatre in the world.

Closed in 1981 for extensive renovations, the opera house was re-opened in all its former magnificence on 27 September 1984: exactly one hundred years after the first performance was given here.

The box office is open between 10:00A.M. and 7:00P.M. daily; seats are usually available on the day of a performance but you may get a seat without a view of the stage! Visits to the Opera House outside of performance hours can only be made with organised groups: contact the tourist office or The Society for Scientific Information (tel: 1431 360) for further information.

## WHAT TO SEE

◆◆◆
### ANDRÁSSY ÚT (NÉPKÖZTÁRSASÁG ÚTJA)/ OKTOGON (NOVEMBER 7 TÉR)/ KODÁLY KÖRÖND

In the days of Franz Josef this elegant avenue, then named after the statesman, Andrássy, was the most fashionable promenading route in Budapest. At one time known as Stalin Avenue, it was until recently called the Avenue of the People's Republic. It runs all the way from Deák tér to Városliget (City Park). The first section was built in the 1870s for rich citizens and prosperous businessmen, whose inflated tastes are reflected in the variety of rather ponderous architectural styles.

**Állami operaház (The Opera House)**, No. 22, was designed by the famous 19th-century Hungarian architect, Miklós Ybl in neo-Renaissance style. It has recently undergone major restoration to celebrate its 100th anniversary. Opposite is the State Ballet School.

**Oktogon (November 7 tér)** is the first major intersection. Originally called Octagon Square in the days when a blue flag flying from the mast of the Skating Club meant that the lake in the City Park was sufficiently frozen over for skating, it was renamed after Mussolini from 1938 to 1945 and until recently commemorated the Russian Revolution. At No. 60, is the former headquarters of the secret police where victims of the Stalinist terror, and later of the Hungarian uprising, were taken to be interrogated and tortured.

**The Liszt Ferenc Zeneművészeti Főiskola (Academy of Music)** is across the road at No. 67. The Hungarian composer Ferenc (Franz) Liszt, of *Hungarian Rhapsody* fame, lived here as its first director from 1881 until his death five years later. The building is in Art Nouveau style, with a statue of Liszt above the main entrance. **The Állami Bábszínház (State Puppet Theatre)** and the **Képzőművészeti Főiskola (Academy of Fine Arts)** occupy the buildings at Nos. 69–71. **Kodály körönd**, an elegant square composed of four neo-Renaissance palaces in a leafy setting, is named after Zoltán Kodály (1882–1967), composer, music researcher and teacher who lived at No. 89.

In the days before World War I, the villas of the final, tree-lined section of the Avenue were the exclusive preserve of the richest Hungarians, including members of the Magyar aristocracy. (The British Consulate was also here.) For the remainder of Andrássy út (Népköztársaság útja) see **Hősök tere (Heroes' Square)** and **Városliget (City Park)**.

◆
### ÁRPÁD HÍD (ÁRPÁD BRIDGE)

The longest of the six bridges crossing the Danube in the vicinity of downtown Budapest, it links the mainland with Margit-sziget (Margaret Island).

◆◆
### BELVÁROSI TEMPLOM (INNER CITY PARISH CHURCH)
*Március 15 tér*

**March 15 Square** (the Revolution of 1848 began on that day) is situated at the Pest end of

*A corner of Kodály körönd*

**Elizabeth Bridge**. This was the centre of the 4th-century Roman settlement of Contra-Aquincum. A small museum exhibits some of the remains. Right next to the overpass you will find one of the most attractive buildings in the city, the so-called Inner City Parish Church. Dating from the 12th century, it is also the oldest. However, it was rebuilt in the 14th century and again, after a fire, in the 18th century. This explains the baroque façade and interior. At one time, the Turks used it as a mosque and you can still see a Muslim prayer niche or *mihrab* to the right of the high altar.

### DOHÁNY UTCA (JEWISH DISTRICT)

At the intersection of Dohány utca and Tanács körút (Metro line 2 Astoria), at the heart of the old Jewish quarter, is the recently restored Synagogue (the largest in Europe). The style of this 19th-century building is Moorish–Byzantine (note the minaret-style towers). The **Zsidó Múzeum (Jewish Museum)** (see below) is here. The streets running between Dohány utca and Dob utca (Síp, Kazinczy,

## WHAT TO SEE

Nagy Diófa, Rumbach, Klauzál tér) are a living memorial to the once-thriving community which was persecuted during World War II. Bullet marks scar the walls of the grimy apartment blocks which also bear Hebrew plaques and tablets commemorating the thousands of families who perished here. (Many of the survivors owe their lives to the Swedish diplomat, Raoul Wallenberg, who worked fearlessly on their behalf before disappearing into a Soviet labour camp at the end of the war.) The entrance ways and courtyards are worth exploring for their period flavour but one cannot help walking away in a sombre frame of mind. Budapest's seventh district (once the most crowded in the entire city) is very much a working class area and Dob utca contains a number of humble but welcoming *étterems* (restaurants) and bars which provide an interesting window onto everyday urban life.

◆
### ERZSÉBET HÍD (ELIZABETH BRIDGE)

This bridge is named after the much-loved Empress Elizabeth, the wife of Franz Josef, who was murdered by an anarchist in 1898. The first bridge, built at the turn of the century, was destroyed during World War II. Its replacement, a modern suspension bridge completed in 1964, owes nothing to the original design.

◆◆
### FÖL DALATTI VASÚTI MÚZEUM (UNDERGROUND RAILWAY MUSEUM)

*Deák tér*

Hidden away in the metro station underpass, the museum occupies one of the original railway tunnels. A fascinating array of plans, drawings, models and carriages traces the development of the first underground system on the European mainland. The first

line, completed in 1896, ran the
entire length of Andrássy
Avenue (Népköztársaság útja), a
distance of two miles (3.5km).
*Open:* Tuesday to Sunday
10:00A.M.–6:00P.M.
*Closed:* Monday

#### ◆◆
GYÓGYFŰRDŐ (THERMAL
BATHS)
For 2,000 years the mineral
waters of the hills around
Budapest have been
appreciated for their therapeutic
effects and today the hot springs
are enjoyed as much as ever
(see **How to be a Local**).
Architecturally, the baths make
some of Budapest's greatest
monuments, and even if you do
not 'take the waters', it is worth
taking a look at some of the
buildings. Bathhouses such as
the **Király** (Fő út), **Császár** (35
Frankel Leó út), **Lukács** (25–9
Frankel Leó út) and **Rudas** (9
Döbrentei tér) survive from the
Turkish period of the 16th and

*Elizabeth Bridge, and Buda beyond*

17th centuries. The popular
**Gellért** baths (Gellért tér) are
housed in a splendid Art
Nouveau building dating from
the early 20th century, the same
period as the elegant **Széchenyi**
baths in Állatkerti körut.

#### ◆
HOPP FERENC KELET-ÁZSIAI
MÚZEUM/KINA MÚZEUM (HOPP
FERENC EASTERN ASIAN
MUSEUM)
*Andrássy út (Népköztársaság
útja) 103 and Gorkij fasor 12*
In two separate premises, the
museum houses the oriental
treasures amassed by the
Hungarian traveller, Ferenc
Hopp (1833–1919) who once
lived here. The Chinese exhibits
are housed in the Ráth György
extension a short walk away.
*Open:* Tuesday to Sunday
10:00A.M.–6:00P.M.
*Closed:* Monday
*Metro:* Kodály körönd (line 1)

### HŐSÖK TERE (HEROES' SQUARE)

A millenary extravaganza, the central feature of Heroes' Square is a 118ft (36m) high column, surmounted by a statue of the Archangel Gabriel; it was supposedly as a result of his intervention that Pope Sylvester II sent a crown to King Stephen. Circling the pedestal are seven figures on horseback, representing the chieftains of the seven Magyar tribes who overran Hungary in 896. The statues which stand in between the columns of the surrounding colonnade honour major figures in the nation's history, including King Stephen and Kossuth. Below each statue is a relief illustrating some significant scene from the life of the person above. After World War II the statues of the Hapsburg rulers were replaced by the Hungarian champions of freedom.

The four groups of symbolic figures on the top of the colonnade represent Work and Wealth, War, Peace and Knowledge and Glory. In front of the monument stands a vast stone tablet: the Hungarian War Memorial, which bears the

*The monument in Heroes' Square*

inscription 'In memory of the heroes who sacrificed their lives for our nation's freedom and for national independence.' The square used to be park-like with trees and bushes; now it boasts ornamental paving, originally laid out in 1938 for the 34th International Eucharistic Congress. The open area adjoining Heroes' Square is known as Procession Square: mass meetings, processions and parades are held here on national and public holidays. It was the site of a monolithic statue of Stalin but during the 1956 revolution this was dragged away, smashed and set alight—a frenzied reassertion of Hungarian nationalism which was captured on contemporary newsreel. Today, Soviet soldiers are among those who pay their respects at the War Memorial. The two neo-classical buildings overlooking the square are the **Szépművészti Múzeum (Fine Arts Museum)** (see entry) and the **Exhibition Hall**.

◆
### IPARMŰVÉSZETI MÚZEUM (MUSEUM OF APPLIED ARTS)
*Üllői út 33–7*
The original building was one of hundreds hastily erected to mark the millenial celebrations of 1896. It was destroyed during World War II and rebuilt in the 1950s. Designed by Ödön Lechner and Gyula Pártos, the coloured ceramic and brick building blends an Art Nouveau style with Hungarian folk motifs. The interior is also fine, with a glass-roofed hall supported by white crenellated arches. There are separate collections of

furniture, metalwork, textiles, woodwork, ceramics and glass, leatherwork, books and paper and other handicrafts.
*Open:* Tuesday to Sunday 10:00A.M.–6:00P.M.
*Closed:* Monday
*Metro:* Ferenc körút (line 3)

◆
### KÖZLEKEDÉSI MÚZEUM (TRANSPORTATION MUSEUM)
*Városliget körut 11, Városliget*
You can combine a visit here with a stroll across the Városliget (City Park). Ideal for younger visitors, the exhibits include models of ships, cars, trains, motorbikes, aeroplanes and engines. An old railway dining car now serves as a restaurant.
*Open:* Tuesday to Sunday 10:00A.M.–6:00P.M.
*Closed:* Monday
*Trolleybus:* 72 from Bajcsy-Zsilinszky

◆◆
### MAGYAR NEMZETI MÚZEUM (HUNGARIAN NATIONAL MUSEUM)
*Múzeum körút*
From the steps of the museum the 19th-century poet, Sándor Petőfi, proclaimed his 'National Song', an event which heralded the 1848 revolution. Arranged to trace the history of Hungary and its peoples, the exhibits of every shape, size and type include prehistoric tools and implements, items dating from the period of the Turkish occupation and memorabilia from the time of the 1848–9 War of Independence. Pride of place, however, (at least in Hungarian eyes) belongs to the exhibition of Hungarian Royal Regalia, including the 11th-century crown

of St Stephen, presented by Pope Sylvester II. Note the crooked cross which appears on the Hungarian coat of arms, currently enjoying a revival.

*Open:* Tuesday to Sunday 10:00 A.M.–6:00 P.M.
*Closed:* Monday
*Metro:* Kálvin tér (line 3)

### MARGIT HÍD (MARGARET BRIDGE)

The original bridge, built to a French design from 1872 to 1876, was destroyed in 1944. It connects with the south end of Margit-sziget (Margaret Island).

### MARGIT-SZIGET (MARGARET ISLAND)

The Island of Hares, as it was once known, was a Royal Game reserve at the time of the Árpád dynasty. It was for centuries the home of various monastic orders and tradition has it that Béla IV vowed during the Mongol invasion that he would bring his daughter up as a nun if his armies were victorious.

Margaret, his daughter, was duly sent to the order of Dominican nuns which prospered under Béla's patronage. She was nine when she went to live on the Island of Hares and she stayed there until she died in 1271. The island took her name at the end of the 19th century; she was canonised in 1943.

During the Turkish occupation many of the buildings on the island were destroyed; it then became the home of the nuns of St Clare and later passed into the hands of the Archduke Palatine Alexander. When Palatine

*Margaret Island: quiet gardens ...*

*... and open-air theatre*

Joseph took over the island in 1795 he planted it with vines and rare trees. In 1869 it was opened to the people as a public park—accessible only by boat until 1876 when Margit híd (Margaret Bridge) was built. In 1908 the city bought the island and visitors were charged an entrance fee which doubled on Sundays and holidays. This kept the island rather exclusive until 1945 when the island was declared a free public park for all citizens.

For the contemporary visitor it remains one of the most unspoilt and peaceful parts of Budapest, a haven for those seeking refuge from the hustle and bustle of urban life. Private cars can be driven on to the island only from the Árpád Bridge (built in 1950) and then only as far as the parking lot next to the Grand Hotel, but many parts of the island can be reached by bus or taxi. You can also hire tricycles (for adults *and* children) from here.
Interesting places to visit include the Alfréd Hajós swimming pool

*The Western Railway Station, an architectural sensation when it was built, and still formidable*

(open to the public on weekends), the ruins of a Franciscan church and, near by, the remains of the Palatines' villa. The ruins of the Dominican nunnery where St Margaret spent most of her life can be visited on the east side of the island. St Michael's Chapel is built on the site of the church of the Premonstratensian monastery; it boasts Hungary's oldest bell, dating from the 15th century, which was discovered under the roots of an upended tree in 1914. On the west side of the island are the Palantinus Baths, perhaps the island's chief attraction in summer: several swimming pools of different temperatures, including one with artificial waves, are set in tree-studded parkland; single-sex terraces are set aside for sunbathing.

Margaret Island is said to be the inspiration for the magic garden in Wagner's opera *Parsifal* and

flavour and are frequented by the wealthy. Near by is the peaceful and charming Japanese Water Garden. There is another open-air theatre used for performances by the Hungarian National Folk Ensemble near the Grand Hotel Car Park.

The Unification Monument is near the Margaret Bridge access. This celebrates the hundredth anniversary of the coming together of Pest, Buda and Óbuda; it was erected in 1972 and designed by István Kiss. Behind it there is a fountain which is colourfully lit at night. In the centre of the island there are huge chestnuts, planes, oaks and acacia – many of them centuries old; willows and rare tulip trees are set on well-kept lawns. Lining the paths are busts of Hungary's most famous writers, artists and composers. János Arany, Hungary's great national poet (1817–1882) used to compose his verses in the shade of these ancient trees. The Casino Restaurant and café are located on the bank of the island facing Pest.

*Bus:* 26 from Marx tér
*Cars:* restricted access only

◆◆
**MARX TÉR AND TERÉZ KÖRÚT (LENIN KÖRÚT)**

One of the city's major traffic intersections, Marx tér is also the home of Budapest's most modernistic shopping complex, the Skála Metró. Opposite is the handsome iron and glass façade of the Nyugati pályaudvar (Western Railway Station), built by the Eiffel company of Paris in the 1870s, before they went on to build the tower. On nearby Váci

the amphitheatre, with the capacity to seat 3,500 people, continues the island's operatic associations. It is the open-air theatre of the State Opera House and opera and ballet performances are staged throughout the summer. The vast stage is surrounded by ancient trees and overlooked by the Water Tower, built in 1911. The north end of the Island (by the Árpád Bridge) contains the Grand Hotel and beyond is the modern Hotel Thermal; both hotels have a cosmopolitan

*The ultra-modern shopping complex, Skálá Metró at Marx tér*

út is the glitzy Westend Shopping Center, selling non-stop hamburgers, jeans, sweatshirts etc.

Running east from Marx tér are the stately Teréz körút and Erzsébet körút (formerly Lenin körút). Nos. 9–11, near Dohány utca, is the **New York Café**. Also known as the **Hungária**, this was the favourite haunt of Budapest's artistic set and is well worth a visit. At the height of its popularity in the 1910s and again in the late 1920s and early 1930s, the café was open 24 hours a day and provided the writers who patronised it (mainly on credit) with free paper and ink. Journals were edited here and caricatures of the editors still hang on the walls. It has been restored to its original glory.

### ◆◆
### MÚZEUM KÖRÚT AND BRÓDY SÁNDOR UTCA

As the name implies, the building dominating Múzeum körút is the neo-classical **Magyar Nemzeti Múzeum (Hungarian National Museum)** (see separate entry). On 15 March 1848, the great poet, Sándor Petőfi, read out his 'National Song' from the

October 1956, secret police guards fired on protesters, initiating the Hungarian uprising.
*Metro:* Astoria (line 2) or Kalvintér (line 3)

◆
### NÉPRAJZI MÚZEUM (ETHNOGRAPHICAL MUSEUM)
*Kóssuth Lajos tér 12*
The sculptures of legislators, magistrates and goddesses of justice which adorn the façade of this late 19th-century building (its architect, Alajos Hauszmann) are explained by the fact that it was formerly the Palace of Justice. Inside it is no less imposing: the enormous entrance hall with marble stairways and huge chandeliers is the setting for a fine fresco by Károly Lotz (look up, it is on the ceiling) showing Justitia, the Goddess of Justice sitting on her throne among the clouds. By her side the groups of allegorical figures represent Justice and Peace (on her right) and Sin and Revenge (on her left).
Permanent exhibitions here include a diverse collection of ethnological material from all over the world; items range from Eskimo furs and kayaks to carved Melanesian masks. Perhaps the most interesting displays are those illustrating the Hungarian peasants' way of life, culture and art. These displays are often supplemented by lively temporary exhibitions. Work tools, ornaments, costumes and 'room sets' all give the visitor a vivid picture.
*Open:* Tuesday to Sunday 10:00A.M.–6:00 P.M
*Closed:* Monday
*Metro:* Kossuth tér (line 2)

top of the steps, an event which marked the beginning of the revolution of that year. The anniversary is now a public holiday and colourful celebrations take place outside. The monument in front of the museum commemorates another 19th-century poet, János Arany, and the adjoining garden contains more monuments to distinguished Hungarians, including Count Széchenyi and the poet/dramatist, Kisfaludy.
**Bródy Sándor utca** is the street immediately to the left of the museum. The ornate yellow building at No.7 is the former radio station from where, on 23

*Népstadion, venue for soccer matches and rock concerts*

◆
## NÉPSTADION

Hungary's largest stadium was opened in 1953 and has a seating capacity of more than 73,000 spectators. It is now part of an extensive sports complex which includes a hotel, a sports museum and various stadia and sports halls.
*Metro:* Népstadion (line 2)

◆
## ÖNTÖDEI MÚZEUM (FOUNDRY MUSEUM)

*Bem József utca 20*
On the site of the 19th-century Ganz ironworks, which produced the world's first electric railway engine, the museum contains a reconstructed wooden foundry and workshop, as well as an interesting collection of the products once manufactured here.
*Open:* Tuesday to Sunday 10:00A.M.–5:00P.M.
*Closed:* Monday
*Metro:* Batthyány tér (line 2)

◆◆◆
## ORSÄGHAZ (PARLIAMENT)

For hundreds of years the Hungarian National Assembly had no permanent address. When a new Parliament building was projected back in the 1880s, the then Prime Minister, Kálmán Tisza, declared: 'There must be no place for caution, calculation and thrift.' Imre Steindl, the architect, followed this directive to the letter and produced an edifice of genuine magnificence which was, at the time of its completion in 1902, the largest and most lavish Parliament building in the world. Work on the building began in 1885; Steindl died in 1902 a few weeks before the building was functioning.
Eclectic in style, but predominantly neo-Gothic in flavour (London's Palace of Westminster is an obvious source of inspiration), it stands guard over the Széchenyi embankment and the river running beneath. The height of the dome (315feet/96m) is an

*The Parliament building, from Buda*

oblique reference to the foundation of the Magyar kingdom (AD 896)—**Szent István Basilika (St Stephen's Basilica)**, which rises near by, is identical in height. Eighty-eight statues adorn the façade, which stretches for a total length of 293 yards (268m). There are nearly 700 rooms, approached by 27 entrances. Ninety pounds (41 kg) of 24 carat gold were required for the gilding.

Of the 88 statues on the exterior, those on the Danube side are the Hungarian rulers, from the seven conquering chiefs to Ferdinand V, who died in 1848. On the Kossuth side are the princes of Transylvania and several famous commanders; above the ground floor windows are the coats of arms of kings and princes.

The main entrance leads to a vast ceremonial staircase which in turn leads to a 16-sided hall beneath the dome, used for official receptions and

*St Stephen's Basilica*

*Food shop in Rákóczi út*

ceremonies. The National
Assembly meets, several times a
year, in the south wing which
boasts an abundance of neo-
Gothic ornamentation; as does
the Congress Hall in the north
wing (where the Upper House
formerly met). Renovations
began in 1925 and have not yet
been finished.

Visitors should look out for some
fine paintings, frescos, and
tapestries by Mihály Munkácsy,
Károly Lotz and Gyula Rudnay.
Perhaps the most notable
painting is Munkácsy's *The
Magyar Conquest*, painted in
1893.

You can visit Parliament only as
part of a group tour (book
through IBUSZ).

Lajos Kossuth (1802–94), after
whom Parliament Square is
named, was a leading instigator
of the 1848 revolution. A member

of the council which ousted the
monarchy and declared
Hungary a republic, he was
forced to flee the country when
the Austrians regained control.
He died in Turin but his body
was brought back to Budapest,
where his funeral was
accompanied by three days of
mourning.

*Metro:* Kossuth tér (line 2)

◆
**PETŐFI HÍD (PETŐFI BRIDGE)**
Named after Hungary's greatest
poet, the revolutionary hero,
Sándor Petőfi (1823–49), the
bridge dates from the 1930s.

◆◆
**RÁKÓCZI ÚT**
One of the main shopping
streets and with a less obviously
Western orientation than some
others, Rákóczi út runs from
Múzeum körút as far as Baross
tér and the Keleti pályaudvar

(Eastern Railway Station). Of the many famous Hungarians called Rákóczi, the one this street is named after was an 18th-century hero, Prince Ferenc Rákóczi II. The Verseny Áruház department store, one of the oldest in Budapest, stands at the corner of Síp utca.

The **Dohány utca** (Jewish **District**) (see entry) runs off to the left. The somewhat sleazy run of pizza bars, well-stocked clothes and electronic shops, beer bars and restaurants (including a Tuborg bar on the corner of Gyulai Pál) continues past the major intersection at

*Hungarian Television building*

Blaha Lujza tér where there is a
metro. At the end of Rákóczi út,
on the left-hand side near the
flyover, is the rather soulless
Grand Hotel Hungaria. Much
more impressive is the façade of
the **Keleti pályaudvar (Eastern
Railway Station)** (built 1881–4)
which you can see ahead. On
either side of the station
entrance are statues of the
British engineers George
Stephenson and James Watt.
*Metro:* Astoria or Keleti
pályaudvar (line 2)

◆
**SZABADSÁG HÍD (FREEDOM
BRIDGE)**
Another postwar reconstruction,
this is on the site of an earlier

*Eastern Railway Station façade*

bridge named after the Emperor
Franz Josef.

◆◆
**SZABADSÁG TÉR**
Szabadság or Freedom Square is
a vast open space in the centre
of the city between **Orsághaz
(Parliament)** and **Szent István
basilika (St Stephen's Basilica)**
(see entries). It was laid out by
Antal Pálóczy in 1902. Three
noteworthy buildings overlook
the Square. On the west side is
the former Stock Exchange, now
**Hungarian Television
Headquarters**. Opposite and
dating from the same period (*c*
1905) is the **National Bank**. The

attractive cream-coloured building with the wrought-iron balconies (on the corner of Perczel utca) is the **American embassy**. The Hungarian Roman Catholic prelate, Cardinal Mindszenty, took refuge here during the 1956 uprising and was persuaded to leave only 15 years later. In the centre of the square there is a small children's playground.

*Széchenyi (Chain) Bridge, a famous Budapest landmark*

◆
### SZÉCHENYI LÁNCHÍD (CHAIN BRIDGE)

The most famous of Budapest's bridges was a wholly British venture, designed by an Englishman and built by a Scotsman, both coincidentally named Clark. The designer, William Tierney Clark, was also responsible for Hammersmith Bridge in London. The first permanent link between Buda and Pest, the Chain Bridge was completed in 1849, against the

wishes of the Austrians, who had tried to blow it up during the War of Independence!

◆
### SZENT ISTVÁN BASILIKA (ST STEPHEN'S CHURCH)

This monstrous edifice was designed by three architects, József Hild, Miklós Ybl and József Kauser, and completed in 1905 but only after the original dome had collapsed following a storm. It now serves as one of the city's major landmarks. The vast interior, which can hold more than 8,000 worshippers, is lavishly decorated with works of art by distinguished Hungarians, including Alajos Stróbl and Károly Lotz, who designed the mosaics inside the dome. St Stephen's right hand is displayed in the Szent Jobb Kápolna (Chapel of the Holy Right Hand) behind the high altar.
*Metro:* Bajcsy-Zsilinszky út (line 1)

## WHAT TO SEE

◆◆◆

### SZÉPMŰVÉSZETI MÚZEUM (FINE ARTS MUSEUM)

*Hősök tere (Heroes' Square)*
On the north side of Heroes' Square stands the Fine Arts Museum; a must for lovers of Western European art, it is one of the major galleries in Central Europe. The building was designed by Albert Schickedanz and Fűlőp Herzog, who were also the architects of the Exhibition Hall (Műscarnok) on the other side of the square (temporary art exhibitions are displayed here).

The Fine Arts Museum has been undergoing restoration since 1987 and this work is expected to carry on well into the 1990s; it is therefore impossible to describe the lay-out of the exhibitions, which are constantly on the move as dictated by the renovations, and you will have to explore as best you can.
Undoubtedly, the collection of Spanish School paintings is the jewel in the museum's crown. There are half a dozen El Grecos as well as works by Goya, Murillo and Veláquez. Other Old Masters worth hunting down in the galleries cover a representative collection of 13th- to 18th-century European painting and include works by Titian, Rembrandt, Raphael, Brueghel, Rubens, Van Dyck and Dürer. British painting is represented by works from Hogarth, Reynolds and Gainsborough. The core of the Old Masters collection came from Miklós Esterházy and was later added to by Károly Pulszky, a notable director of the museum. Pulszky, however,
enraged the government of the day by his lack of interest in the work of contemporary Hungarian artists; he was dismissed and eventually committed suicide in Australia. Strong on the French Impressionists and Post Impressionists, the modern foreign collection has, among others, works by Delacroix, Courbet, Millet, Gauguin, Monet, Renoir, Cézanne and Toulouse-Lautrec. Of the 20th-century artists, Picasso, Chagall, Kokoschka, Le Corbusier, and Vasarely are all represented. The museum has a vast holding of prints and drawings, which include works by Dürer, Rembrandt and Leonardo da Vinci. While the restoration work is in progress, a selection of these are periodically shown only in temporary displays.
At present, most of the collection of European sculpture (mainly Italian and 17th- to 18th-century baroque work) is in storage; there are, however, some pieces displayed in various parts of the museum. Ancient Egyptian art is also represented here in a small but rich collection which includes painted wooden mummy cases, reliefs from the wall of a temple built during the 4th century BC and statuary. The Graeco-Roman collection is of international importance and there are many fine examples of ceramics dating from the 6th to the 1st century BC.
*Open:* Tuesday to Sunday 10:00A.M.–6:00P.M.
*Closed:* Monday
*Metro:* Hősök tere

**The Fine Arts Museum**

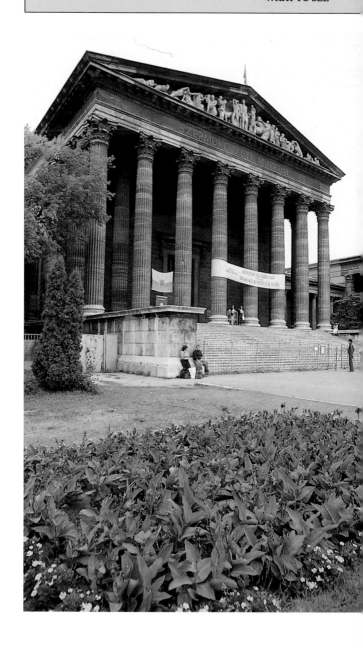

◆◆◆
**VÁROSLIGET (CITY PARK)** *City
Park Area*
Until the beginning of the 19th
century this was nothing but a
bare, open space. At the turn of
the present century it was laid
out as a park to complement the
elegant new villas that were
sprouting along Andrássy út. It is
a popular resort for Pestian
dwellers even today—part
wooded and partly given over to
entertainments of a more man-
made nature. The City Park is
the biggest of its kind in
Budapest and was the chosen
site for the great Millenary
Exhibition in 1896, held to
commemorate a thousand years
of the Hungarian State. In all,
over 200 halls and pavilions
were erected and the country's
first museum village was built to
represent the lives of the
peasants. Of course many of

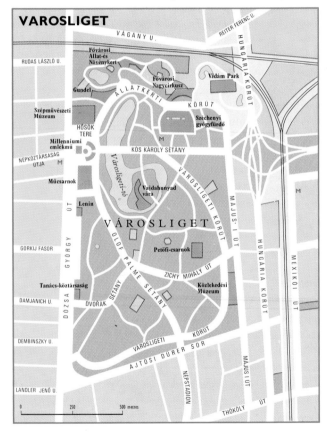

these buildings were dismantled after the exhibition was ended, but a few remain.

Standing on an island in the boating lake is **Vajdahunyad Vara (Castle)** set amongst a group of trees. The castle was built for the exhibition. It was designed by the architect Ignác Alpár, and reflects a hodgepodge of architectural styles: Romanesque, Gothic, Transitional and Renaissance-baroque. Part of the castle was modelled on a castle of the same name which stands near Hunedoara in Romania; the original has become a casualty of the Ceaucescu regime and has been left to fall into decline. In all, 22 buildings were used as models for Budapest's Vajdahunyad and perhaps surprisingly, given the variety of styles, it is pleasing to the eye, giving the impression of a fairy-tale castle. Opposite the main entrance is a statue of Anonymus, the first medieval Hungarian chronicler. The entrance to the Museum of Agriculture is found in the baroque wing of the castle and so too is the Museum of Natural Sciences (*Open:* daily except Monday 10:00A.M.–6:00P.M. In winter early closing on weekdays at 5:00P.M.).

As well as an open-air skating rink (in winter only) City Park has a variety of other attractions and places to visit.

The **Fővárosi Allat-és Növénykert (Municipal Zoological and Botanical Gardens)** opened in 1866. They were founded by a member of the Academy of Sciences, János Xantus, a natural scientist who

spent a great deal of time in the United States. The zoo boasts some impressive examples of the city's Art Nouveau heritage, for example the main gate, which is supported by four stone elephants. Currently the zoo is undergoing renovations to improve the accommodation for the 4,000 animals that live there. Budapest Zoo, one of Central Europe's oldest, boasts an international reputation for the high fertility rate of its hippopotami (which do not usually breed well in captivity) —this is apparently due to the constant supply of thermal spring water.

Next to the zoo is the **Fővárosi Nagycirkusz (Municipal Circus)** (tel: 428-300 for details of performances.) The first circus in Pest, the Hetz Theatre was built on the site of the Lutheran Church in Deák tér. A permanent circus was then built on the present-day site although the building which stands now dates only from the early 1970s. Beyond the circus is the amusement park; the traditional merry-go-round and the wooden roller coaster are pre-war. There are, however, plenty of more modern rides plus a small children's playground between the circus and the amusement park.

The **Széchenyi gyógyfürdő (Baths)** are found opposite the circus. They were designed in 1909 and enlarged in 1926 to incorporate an open-air swimming pool and medicinal pools fed by thermal springs. This is one of the largest buildings of its kind in Europe. The Medicinal Baths, which were designed by Győző Czigler and Ede Dvozsák between 1909 and 1913, has a huge Art Nouveau mosaic inside the dome of the building; all the fittings from the tiles on the floor to the light fixtures are perfect period pieces. The northern wing of the building, with its neo-baroque interior, was designed by Imre Francsek. Here you will find regular visitors playing chess on floating cork chessboards whilst they sit in the thermal pools; there is also a lively restaurant with a view

*Vajdahunyad Castle, in City Park*

of the thermal pools so you can sit and watch this spectacle. Opposite the entrance to the baths is a statue of engineer and geologist, Vilmost Zsigmond, who discovered the first medicinal springs in the park in 1877.

Towards the southeast corner of the park at Majus 1. út 26 is the **Közlekedési Múzeum (Transportation Museum)** (see entry) and near by is the charming Garden for the Blind, especially designed to be appreciated by those with impaired sight.

The Museum of Transportation's Exhibition of Air and Space Travel is located at a different venue, also in City Park: Petőfi Hall was rebuilt in 1985 on the site of an old exhibition hall and is now Budapest's main Youth Centre and the 'stronghold' of Hungarian rock and pop music. It is also the venue for a flea market, theatrical performances for children, a roller-skating club and is popular for dancing on Saturday evenings.

The statue of George Washington located here was funded by the Hungarian immigrants who arrived in the United States between 1871 and 1913.

◆
**VÁSÁRCSARNOK (CENTRAL MARKET HALL)**
*Dimitrov tér*
*At the time of writing, due to close for renovation.*
The square, at the Pest end of the Szabadsághid (Freedom Bridge), is named—for how much longer, one wonders—after Georgi

Dimitrov, a hero of the Bulgarian socialist movement. The vast neo-gothic hall was completed in 1896. Fruit, vegetables, meat and fish predominate but you can also buy artwork and handicrafts.

◆
**VIGADÓ TÉR to ROOSEVELT TÉR**
This part of downtown Budapest is largely a late 19th-century development. The central feature of Vigadó tér is the **Vigadó kulturközpont (Concert Hall)**, designed in the 1860s by Frigyes Feszl. The richly decorated exterior gives the building its distinguished look, but the interior foyer, staircase and halls are more pleasing to the eye. (The frescos have recently been restored.) Liszt, Wagner and Mahler are among those who have performed here. **Roosevelt tér**, formerly Chain Bridge Square, was named after the US President, F D Roosevelt, in 1947. On either side of the square are monuments to the 19th-century statesmen, Ferenc Deák, author of the famous Compromise of 1867, and Count István Széchenyi (1791–1860), one-time Minister of Transportation and a leading social and economic reformer. At the northern end of Roosevelt tér is the **Magyar Tudormányos Académia (Hungarian Academy of Sciences)**, designed by the German architect, F A Stuler.
*Metro:* Vörösmarty tér (line 1)

◆◆◆
**VÖRÖSMARTY TÉR and VÁCI UTCA**
This charming and restful square (now pedestrianised) is named

## WHAT TO SEE

after the 19th-century Romantic poet, Mihály Vörösmarty (1800–55), whose monument stands in the centre. On the north side, at No.7, is the famous **Gerbeaud pastry shop**, named after the Swiss, Emil Gerbeaud, who took it over in 1884. **Váci utca**, on the far side of the square, is Budapest's most exclusive shopping street. A mecca for Westerners, the shops here are stocked with all the familiar brand names you thought you had left behind—Estée Lauder, Adidas, Benetton etc. There is a McDonalds (a favourite haunt of street entertainers in the evening) and a rival City Grill. You can have coffee in the Expresso Bar or buy your clothes in La Boutique Suisse. There is a pizza parlour and a whole range of electronic shops selling video equipment and even computers. Look out for the graffiti advertising Pet Shop Boy (sic), Beastie Boys, Sex Pistols etc. Near by, in Szende Pál utca, is the Gösser Disco Bar open until 3:00 A.M.

### ZSIDÓ MÚZEUM (JEWISH MUSEUM)
*Dohány utca 2*
Located in the annexe of the Central Synagogue, in the heart of the Jewish district, the museum traces the history of Hungarian Jewry.
*Open:* mid-May to mid-October; Tuesday, Wednesday, Friday, Sunday 10:00 A.M.–1:00 P.M., Monday and Thursday 2:00–6:00 P.M.
*Closed:* Saturday
*Metro:* Astoria (line 2)

*Monument to Mihály Vörösmarty*

## Around Budapest

### BUDAI-HEGYSÉG (THE BUDA HILLS)

At some point in your stay you will probably feel the need to get away from the fumes and fury of the city. Fortunately, the outskirts of Budapest, especially the woodland to the west, around **Szabadság-hegy (Liberty Hill)**, have much to offer.

The easiest point of access is via the cogwheel railway which runs from Szilágyi Erzsébet fasor, near the Hotel Budapest (bus 22 from Moszkva tér) to Albert utca (Vörös Csillag utca). Here you can pick up the Pioneer Railway, seven and a half miles (11 km) of narrow-gauge track, maintained and administered by smartly uniformed members of the Hungarian youth movement who do everything except drive the trains. There are a number of stops along the route: each has its own attractions, from secluded footpaths and breathtaking views to wayside restaurants and picnic areas. In the winter, you can ski down the slopes of **János-hegy**; the ski lift continues to operate in the summer, taking visitors on a leisurely journey to the summit at 1,735ft (529m) from Zugligeti út. If you want to stray beyond the confines of the railway, buses leave from various points in the centre of town to a host of scenic destinations, including **Hármashatár-hegy** where, from April to the end of October, you can explore the fascinating Pálvölgy and Szemlőhegy stalactite caves. (Buses 65 and 29 respectively run from Kolosy

tér halfway between the Árpád and Margit Bridges. Or you can drive from Kolosy tér along Szép-völgyi út to the summit.)

### THE DANUBE BEND (ESZTERGOM, SZENTENDRE, VISEGRÁD)

About 30 miles (50km) north of Budapest, the River Danube abruptly changes course, meandering south through a beautiful stretch of hilly, unspoilt countryside. The towns of the Danube Bend are easily accessible and well worth visiting.

### Esztergom

Historic Esztergom has been the centre of Hungary's Roman Catholic church since the 11th century. Appropriately the **Basilica**, which dominates Castle Hill, is the largest church in the country. Little remains of the original medieval building, however, and the present structure (designed by József Hild) dates only from the early 19th century. The interior is sumptuous but the main point of interest is the Bakócz Chapel, named after the cardinal who commissioned it in the early 16th century. When the old cathedral was demolished the chapel was reassembled, stone by stone, in its present position. The altar, in white marble, is the work of Florentine craftsmen and was designed by Andrea Ferrucci in 1519. Separate tickets are required to visit the crypt (the burial place of Esztergom's archbishops), the treasury, with its notable collection of precious objects, and the bell-tower from which there is a fine view of the

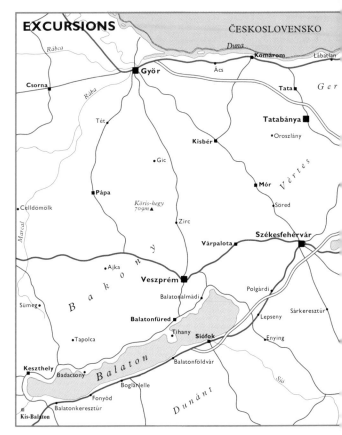

EXCURSIONS

ČESKOSLOVENSKO

Danube and the Pilis Hills.
Before leaving Castle Hill take a
few moments to inspect the ruins
of the **Paloka (old palace)**,
vacated when the court moved
to Buda after the Mongol
invasion. Your main ports of call
should be St Stephen's Hall, the
Hall of Virtues, decorated with
Renaissance wall paintings, and
the 12th-century chapel, with its
distinctive rose window above
the doorway.

On the far side of Bajcsy-
Zsilinszky út is the Primate's
Palace which houses the
**Christian Museum**, a must for art
lovers with its collection of old
Italian masters including works
by Duccio, Lorenzo di Credi and
Giovanni di Paolo. There are also
some outstanding Hungarian and
Bohemian altarpieces. Next door
is the **Oreg-templon (Water
Town Parish Church)**, which
dates from the 18th century.

Architecturally, Esztergom is a
pot-pourri of styles and a stroll
through the Watertown district in
the direction of Széchenyi tér
and the 18th-century Town Hall
will introduce you to baroque,
rococo and classical (and the
various staging posts in
between!). The tourist
information office is also in
Széchenyi tér.
*Bus:* from Erzsébet tér (Engels
tér)

*Boats:* from Vigadó tér
*Cars:* Road 10 or the more
scenic Road 11

**Szentendre**
Szentendre (St Andrew), a treat
for tourists, with its delightful
architecture and relaxed cultural
atmosphere, is a mere 12 miles
(18km) from Budapest. **Fő tér**
(formerly Marx tér) is the focal
point of the town. The ornate
wrought-iron cross in the centre
of the square was erected by
Serbian merchants to
commemorate deliverance
from the plague in 1763. The
Serbs, who began arriving as
refugees from Ottoman Turkey
as early as the 14th century,
came to form a sizeable
community in Szentendre. They
built the **Blagovestenska
(Annunciation) Church** (now a
museum) and the four merchant
houses dating from 1720–30,
which now constitute the **Picture
Gallery**. Paintings, tapestries
and sculptures by members of
the talented **Ferenczy** family can
be found at No. 6 Fő tér, while,
just around the corner, the
**Margit Kovács museum** is
devoted to a collection of her
exquisite modern ceramics.
(*Open:* 9:00A.M.–7:00P.M. daily)
From Fő tér prepare yourself
for a steep climb up **Castle Hill**,
where you will find two more
churches (Serbian Orthodox
and Roman Catholic) and
another small painting museum,
dedicated to the works of the
Impressionist, **Béla Czóbel**.
Tourist Information is at
Bogdányi utca 1.
About two miles (3km)
northwest of the town (catch a
bus from the HÉV terminal on

## WHAT TO SEE

Dunakanyar körut, stand 8) is the open air **Szabadtéri Néprajzi Múzeum (Village Museum)**, an ambitious attempt to evoke the atmosphere of a 19th-century rural community. White-washed peasant houses, thatched roofs, wooden towers, churches, barns, mills etc.

*Open:* April–October
9:00 A.M.–5:00 P.M.
*Closed:* Monday
*HÉV suburban railway:* from Batthyány tér
*Boat:* from Vigadó tér
*Cars:* Road 11

### Visegrád

One of the most picturesque spots on the entire Danube Bend, Visegrád is popular with Hungarians and foreigners alike. The Romans built the first fortified settlement here in the 4th century AD and it was still in use as late as the 10th century. At that time, Visegrád was inhabited by Slavs who gave it its present name, meaning 'lofty fortress'. Work began on the Royal Palace in the 13th century, and a succession of rulers added their own embellishments until King Matthias Corvinus had created what Pope Sixtus IV described as a 'Paradise on earth'. Decline set in after the Turkish occupation and today Visegrád is once more a charming, but sleepy, village.

The tourist route begins at Fő utca, near the landing stage, where there is also a tourist office. So much of the **Palace** was destroyed that doubts were even expressed about its site until excavations began in 1934. They have been going on ever since. At the centre of the ruins,

approached by a reconstruction of the original Gothic arcaded passageway, is the court of honour featuring a pilastered loggia and part of a Renaissance fountain—all that survives of the original palace built by Charles Robert of Anjou early in the 14th century. Near the outer wall, on the terrace, is a copy of the ornate Lion Fountain. The remains of the original can be seen in the **Solomon Tower**, the former keep of the lower castle, situated to the north of the landing stage. Built originally in the 13th and 14th centuries, it is now a **museum** containing various artefacts recovered from the Palace interior—the Hercules Fountain, being the most celebrated. A steep climb

will take you to the **Fellegvár
Citadel**, a superb vantage point
for excellent views and
photographs.
*Coach:* from Erzsébet tér
(Engels tér)
*HÉV suburban railway:* to
Nagymaros, then onward by
ferry
*Boat:* from Vigadó tér (fastest
journey time 50 mins)
*Cars:* Road 11 via Szentendre

◆◆

**LAKE BALATON**
*Approx 60 miles (100 km) from
Budapest*
Hungary's 'seaside' is actually
the largest freshwater lake in
Western Europe, with a
shoreline of more than 125 miles
(200 km) and an area of

*Swimming at Lake Balaton*

230 square miles (595 sq km). All
tastes are catered to here: sports
enthusiasts will enjoy swimming
in temperatures approaching
85°F (30°C) at the height of the
summer and there are facilities
for windsurfing, fishing (there
are over 40 species of fish in the
lake), sailing and bicycling. Or
you can lie out in the sun and
relax on one of the sandy
beaches along the southern
shore. Resorts jostle for space
around the perimeter of the lake
offering shops, restaurants, bars
and even a nightlife of sorts
(though, surprisingly, not many
dance clubs).
The northern shore is the more
attractive: **Balatonalmádi** (brash

and modern with good facilities), **Balatonfüred** (spas, sanatoria and a busy harbour), **Tihany** (rich in history but over-popular), **Badacsony** (striking scenery) and **Keszthely** (bars and restaurants) are the main resorts. **Siófok**, the largest town on the southern shore, is the starting point for local excursions (Siotour, Szabadság tér 6).
*Train:* all destinations from the Southern Railway Station (Déli pályaudvar)
*Cars:* Motorway M7 or Highway 70 or 71 (southwest of city)

◆
### ÓBUDA
The Árpád Bridge crosses the southern tip of Óbuda Island. Most of old Óbuda has been demolished to make way for housing estates and modern

*The Basilica at Esztergom*

high-rises; there are, however, several worthwhile art galleries and enough architecture to give the visitor an idea of its 'turn of the century' atmosphere. Indeed until the Tartar invasions it was the more important of the Buda settlements and only lost its prominence when Béla IV was compelled to flee behind the fortifications on Castle Hill in the mid-13th century. From this time it became known as Old Buda or Óbuda but still retained its royal patronage. The palace, built by Andrew II at the beginning of the 13th century, continued to be occupied by the queens or the royal dowagers under the Angevins; little remains of it now. Virtually nothing remains from the medieval settlements of Óbuda either, but there are remains of its 18th- and 19th-century life. For example,

the **parish church**, built by the local landlords, the Zichy family, in the 1740s has some fine sculptures mainly by Károly Bebó. The restored neo-classical synagogue (in Lajos utca) dates from 1821 and is now a cultural centre; it used to be surrounded by a Jewish ghetto but that has been pulled down. In the **Fő tér (Main Square)** and surrounding streets there are several fine baroque houses; the area has been carefully restored. Zichy Mansion, completed in 1757, on the east side of the square, is the district's **cultural centre**. Its large internal courtyard is used for summer concerts and inside there is a collection of works by painter and writer **Lajos Kassák** (*open:* daily except Monday 10:00A.M.–6:00P.M.). The Óbuda **Local History Collection** is also housed here and this includes a display of barrel-making instruments (*open:* Tuesday to Friday 2:00–6:00P.M., Saturday and Sunday 10:00A.M.–6:00P.M.). On the Korvin Ottó tér (Szenflólek tér) is the **Vasarely Museum**. Victor Vasarely, the founder of Op-Art, donated 400 of his works to the country of his birth. This museum displays a representative selection of his paintings and in addition features a library, lecture hall and often temporary exhibitions of one kind or another (*Open:* daily except Monday 10:00A.M.–5:00P.M.).
In the northeast corner of Fő tér there is the sculpture 'Strollers in the Rain'. The full-size bronze figures of women with umbrellas are the work of Imre Varga, one of the most prolific of

contemporary sculptors. More of his work can be seen at the nearby **Imre Varga Gallery** at 7 Laktanya utca.
Another interesting collection to visit in Óbuda is the **Zsigmond Kun Folk Art Collection**. Zsigmond Kun was a connoisseur and collector of ceramics and folk art; his former home is now a museum and the displays include pottery, textiles, carvings and furniture from all over Hungary. (*Open:* Tuesday to Friday 2:00–6:00P.M.; weekends 10:00A.M.–6:00P.M. *Closed:* Monday.)
The **museum at Kiscelli utca** 108 (formerly a Trinitarian Monastery and set on a wooded hill above the town) houses the modern department of the Budapest Historical Museum. There is a noteworthy collection of 20th-century pictures here but the museum also illustrates the capital's history from the liberation of the city from the Turks (1686) to the present day. *Bus:* 86 to Flórián tér (near Árpád bridge)
*HÉV suburban train:* from Batthyány tér to Aquincum

**Aquincum**
Spread across the Óbuda area is the Roman site of Aquincum. The Romans settled here in the 2nd and 3rd centuries AD and at its zenith the population of Aquincum numbered around 40,000. At first it was mainly a Roman garrison town (about 6,000 soldiers were stationed here); later, as people from all parts of the Empire settled in Aquincum, it became the provincial capital of Pannonia Inferior.

## WHAT TO SEE

The military population lived in the area of what is today the town of Óbuda, the civilian population 2 miles (3 km) to the north, so the remains are somewhat spread out. The general consensus is that it is best to begin a visit to the Roman remains with the ruins of the **Amfiteatrum (Amphitheatre of the Military Town)**. These are located at the corner of Korvin Ottó utca (Szenflólek tér) and Nagyszombat utca (about half a mile (1 km) away from the Flórián tér; buses 84 and 86). The amphitheatre, built in the 2nd century AD had the largest arena north of the Mediterranean capable of seating around 15,000 spectators who would flock to see the lavish, and sometimes bloody, spectacles. In the 4th century the amphitheatre was converted into a fortress; the evidence suggests that from then on battles constantly arose over its ownership. The ruins were discovered in 1937 and excavated until 1939.

The remains of a large villa on Meggyfa utca was probably once the home of a wealthy Imperial official. It is known as the **Hercules Villa** because of its well-preserved mosaic floors, dated to around the beginning of the 3rd century and depicting scenes from the legends of Hercules and Dionysus. These mosaics are among the best Roman remains in Hungary. *Open:* May to October 10:00A.M.–2:00P.M.; Saturday and Sunday 10:00A.M.–6:00P.M. *Closed:* Mondays.

The **Roman Baths Museum** (*Open:* May to August 10:00A.M.–6:00P.M.; September to October 10:00A.M.–3:00P.M. *Closed:* Mondays) has an entrance in the underpass to Flórián tér and indeed the underpass network beneath the square has become a **Roman Settlement Museum** with display cabinets and stone remains. East of Szentendrei út (approx two and a half miles (4 km) north of Flórián tér) is the site of the remains of the **walled civilian town** and the **Aquincum Museum** (*Open:* May to October 10:00A.M.–6:00P.M. *Closed:* Monday). The museum was built in 1894 in neo-classical style to house Roman relics found in the area; its prize exhibit is a rare example of a 3rd-century organ. The remains of the civilian town are set around the museum and a good idea of its layout can be gained. The excavations include the remains of some large public baths, a market place, a temple, a shrine to the Persian sun-god Mithras, dwelling houses and a Christian church. Elsewhere in the area are the ruins of the **civilian amphitheatre**, far smaller than the military amphitheatre with a capacity for only 6,000.
*Buses:* 42 and 34 from Korvin Ottó tér (Szenflólek tér).
*HÉV* suburban railway from Batthyány tér, Buda to Aquincum station.

About half a mile (1 km) from the Aquincum Museum there is the Római Outdoor Swimming Pool and Camping-Site (there is also a motel here). Lukewarm spring water – used for bathing by the Romans – feeds the swimming pools in one of the loveliest outdoor swimming areas of the city, set in open fields.

## PEACE AND QUIET

### Wildlife and Countryside in and around Budapest

#### by Paul Sterry

Whether you have an interest in natural history, or simply enjoy the peace and quiet of forests, lakesides or the countryside as a whole, Hungary has a great deal to offer. There are plenty of sites within easy access of Budapest itself for quiet contemplation. Hungary is a landlocked country, bordered to the north by Czechoslovakia and the Ukraine (formerly USSR), to the west by Austria, to the south by Yugoslavia and to the east by Romania. Within its compara-tively small area (roughly 300 miles (483 km) wide and 150 miles (240 km) across) are flat, fertile plains, extensive lakes, forests, hills and mountains. Much of lowland Hungary is agricultural land, and the country is famous for its fruit and vegetable production. This land-use has all but eliminated the natural grassland landscape that once comprised the Alföld (Great Hungarian Plain) to the south and east of Budapest. However, here and there pockets of this habitat remain and many of the creatures associated with it manage to survive in the modern, man-made agricultural landscape.

### In and Around Budapest

To get the most from a visit, it is probably best to rent a car and explore the country at a slow pace. However, those visitors on a short visit to the capital can still find plenty of wildlife interest near by. There are parks and gardens with interesting birds in the middle of Budapest and forests and hills lie on the outskirts. The following are some of the more interesting sites for visitors seeking peace and quiet and with an interest in natural history.

### Margit-sziget (Margaret Island)

Except for the point of access on Margaret Bridge this haven of tranquillity is cut off from the city

by the waters of the Danube. Private cars are banned from the area and the woodlands are a haven for birds such as woodpeckers and flycatchers. The island is an extremely popular recreational area, with swimming pools, sports grounds and gardens.

## Városliget or City Woodland Park

This park lies to the east of Hősök tere on the east side of the Danube in Pest. The central feature is a replica of Vajdahunyad Castle, surrounded by a man-made moat; there is also a zoo, agricultural museum, transport museum and amusement park. For birdwatchers, the spring and summer months are best in the extensive woodlands here. As with other parks in the city, best results are had by arriving early in the morning and by avoiding weekends and public holidays.

## Budai-hegység (The Buda Hills)

The Buda Hills fringe the western border of Buda and are a delightful area for relaxing strolls in woodland or for birdwatching; they can be reached on bus 65 from Ujlaki Parish Church. Three hills—Hill of the Three Boundaries, St John's Hill and Freedom Hill— dominate the area and there are trails and short ski lifts to allow exploration. Woodland birds, including birds of prey, warblers and woodpeckers, abound. Colourful flowers can be found in bloom in spring and summer while in autumn the woods are renowned for the variety and abundance of fungi

they harbour. Visitors may also wish to see the Budakeski Game Park (bus 22 to Korayi Sanatorium), where wild boar and deer are kept.

## Birds of Budapest's Woodlands

Although the birdlife of the woods can be rather uninteresting in the winter, in spring the resident birds start singing, their numbers boosted by migrant visitors. Listen for the loud, fluty song of the golden oriole. Although males are bright yellow, they are difficult to spot in the dappled foliage and the song is the best clue to their presence. Several species of warblers also arrive in spring; the Bonelli's warbler has a high-pitched trilling song which is sung from high in the branches. Birds of prey circle over the more remote areas of woodland, scanning the ground below for food and advertising their territories. Look out for honey buzzards, which soar on broad, rounded wings that have conspicuous bars on them.

### Flycatchers

Flycatchers are summer visitors to the woods around Budapest. As their name suggests, these delightful birds catch insects, making aerial forays from a prominent perch. Two species are particularly common around the city. The collared flycatcher has black-and-white plumage with a prominent white collar. The red-breasted flycatcher has an orange-red breast and continually pumps its tail up and down.

## Further Afield

Because Budapest is centrally placed in Hungary, many of the best wildlife areas, including national parks and reserves, can be reached in a day. The following are among the best sites.

### Lake Velence

This shallow lake lies about 30 miles (48km) southwest of Budapest and is a popular holiday destination for residents of the capital. Migratory ducks and waders can be seen around the shores, and herons, egrets and warblers breed in the extensive reed-beds that fringe the margins. To reach Lake Velence, take Route 70 to Székesfehérvár—not the M7. The road runs along the southern

*The red-breasted flycatcher*

shores of the lake and visitors should stop at any suitable vantage points. Minor roads run along the eastern and western ends of the lake and fields and marshes should be searched for wading birds.

### Lake Balaton

This huge lake lies southwest of Budapest. The quickest route from the capital is to take the M7; once there, roads run around the entire margin of the lake. Wetland birds can be seen in many undisturbed places around the lake, but the best site is probably the Kis-Balaton Reserve. This small, marshy lake lies between the villages of Vors, Zalavar and Balatonszentgyörgy at the eastern end of Lake

## PEACE AND QUIET

Balaton. It boasts large numbers of breeding wetland birds and has an observation tower. To visit the reserve you need prior permission: contact the **Hungarian Nature Conservation Authority**, H-1121 Budapest, Kolto u21, or enquire at the tourist office in the town of Keszthely. There is a national park on the Tihany peninsula, which juts into the northern shores of Lake Balaton. The volcanic scenery is largely wooded and there are marked trails.

### Birds of the Lakes

Herons and egrets are the most conspicuous of Hungary's lakeland birds. Both little and great egrets breed in the country and can be identified by their all-white plumage. Little egrets have dark bills and black legs with yellow feet. The larger great egret has dark legs and feet and a yellow bill. Spoonbills are superficially similar to egrets: they are roughly the same size and have white plumage. However, they are easily told by their long, spatulate bills. Several species of herons are also found in Hungary's reed-beds and marshes. Most are rather secretive and require patient observation to see them.

### Alföld (The Great Hungarian Plain)

The Great Hungarian Plain lies southeast of Budapest and is bordered to the west by the River Danube, to the north by mountains, and runs southeast to the Romanian and Yugoslavian borders. Although much of the land between the Danube and

---

**White Stork**
The white stork is one of Europe's most familiar birds. It has a tall, heron-like stance and distinctive white plumage with black wings. The legs are reddish, as is the large, heavy bill. Storks often nest on buildings and are welcome visitors; they are considered to be a sign of good luck and a nesting stork confers good fortune on the household. White storks build large, rather untidy nests of twigs and debris which are often used year after year. To induce the birds to nest, people often put old cartwheels or specially made wooden structures on their roofs to serve as bases upon which the birds can build. Storks are summer visitors to Hungary, arriving in April and departing in August and September to spend the winter in Africa.

---

the River Tisza to the east is cultivated, there are pockets of the natural steppe grassland left, together with salt lakes and woodlands, while beyond the Tisza the landscape is more unspoilt.
An introduction to the wildlife of the Great Hungarian Plain can be found less than 30 miles (48km) from the centre of Budapest. Take Route 50 southeast from the capital and turn off at Alsónémed to the town of Ócsa. Here you will find wet meadows and alder carr woodland. Several species of waders breed in the meadows, including black-tailed godwits and redshank, and the woodlands harbour rollers, golden orioles and red-footed falcons.
Continue along the road to

Szeged from the capital and you will find more birds characteristic of the plains. Just before you reach the town, stop to look at Lake Fehér-tó on the east side of the E75. Wildfowl and waders are often abundant here.

The Kiskunság Nemzeti (National) Park comprises six separate areas of steppe land or 'puszta' to the east of Szeged. The administrative centre is at Kecskemét, while the best areas within the park are between Lakitelek and Tőserdő on the Tisza, Fülöpszállás (a bird reserve) and the sand dune area between Bugac and Bocsa. There is a herdsman's museum in Bugac and an agricultural museum in Lajosmimzse.

### The Hortobágy Plain

This is the largest remaining area of steppe grassland left in Hungary and lies between the River Tisza and the town of Debrecen to the east of Budapest. Part of the area is a national park, the headquarters of which are in the village of Hortobágy. Hortobágy is a birdwatcher's paradise, with something to see throughout the year: open country birds including great bustards and birds of prey are often seen and wetland birds breed around the ponds and lakes. Migration time is excellent with ducks, cranes and storks much in evidence. Use the minor roads to explore.

*A white stork on its roof-top nest*

## PEACE AND QUIET

*The threatened great bustard*

### Great Bustard
The Hungarian plains are among the best remaining areas for one of Europe's largest and most threatened birds—the great bustard. They have bulky bodies and long necks and legs and are found only in flat, open country. Males, which are larger than females, are Europe's heaviest bird. In flight they resemble a huge goose, while on the ground they have an upright stance. In the spring, males perform elaborate displays to attract females: they inflate their throats, pull back their necks and fan out white feathers in the tail and wings.

### Gemenci-erdö (The Gemenc Forest)
This forest lies near the town of Baja, south from Budapest on Route 51. It is part of the Danube's floodplain, and is made up of a mosaic of wetlands, marshes and woodlands of different types. The best areas of woodland lie on the west bank of the Danube both to the north and the south of the town. Gemenc is an excellent area for woodland birds, wild boar and deer, but is well worth visiting for its beauty alone. Access to the forest reserve is controlled: visitors can either take boat tours or travel on the small-gauge railway.

### Visegrád
Visegrád lies to the north of Budapest on the south bank of the Danube; it can be reached by taking Route 11 from the capital. The surrounding hills are covered in forests which are excellent for woodland birds, mammals, flowers and fungi. In the vicinity is the Pilis Hills Park, a former Royal hunting ground, which is also good for wildlife.

### Bukki Nemzeti (National) Park
This national park lies on a limestone massif, northeast of Budapest, and has caves, waterfalls and gorges. The extensive forests of beech and oak have been untouched for many years and have exceptionally rich ground flora, including many species of orchids. Not surprisingly, the birdlife is rich and woodland mammals thrive. The administrative centre for the national park is in Miskolc; access to the region is either from Miskolc or from Eger. The most scenic route is along the mountain road between the two towns, which passes through Répáshuta and Bükk-szentkeresz.

## FOOD AND DRINK

### Food

Hungarian food is both rich and filling. It is also fairly heavily meat-based, so vegetarians can be in for a hard time, though you will find, apart from vegetables, some pulse and egg dishes (the word for egg is *tojás*). You should see some fish on most menus. The soup is often a meal in itself. *Gulyás* is chunks of beef with potatoes and vegetables thrown in. Drink it slowly because it is usually very heavily spiced with the ever present paprika. *Halászlé* is a hot fish soup. You may also find *Hortobágyi húsos palacsinta* on the menu. These are pancakes filled with mincemeat and covered in sour cream. Vegetarians may like to look out for *körözött*, a specially prepared ewes' cheese, often served with butter, chives and paprika. For the main course, you are likely to be offered such things as *Balatoni fogas* (pike-perch from Lake Balaton), *fatányéros* (mixed grill), *töltött káposzta* (stuffed cabbage). If you are eating in a fairly suave establishment, you may be offered goose liver, venison, wild boar or other game. Main meals are served either with salad or potatoes. If you have any room left, try *meggyes* (sour cherry), *rétes* (strudel) or *palacsinta* (pancakes) with various fillings.

### Drink

The most famous white wines are known collectively as *Tokaji* from the region in which they are grown. They come in sweet and dry varieties but tend to be a little on the heavy side. If you prefer red wine, try *Egri Bikavér* (bull's blood). The authentic Hungarian spirits are brandies called *pálinka*. There are various flavours: *barack* (apricot), *cseresznye* (cherry) and *szilva* (plum). Vermouth is *ürmös*. The best Hungarian beers are Kőbányai and Dreher, but you will also find Czech Urquell and a large number of foreign brands (Tuborg is very big here). If you are out and about and in need of a drink, the general name for beer is *sör* and for wine, *bor*. A wine bar is *borozó* and a beer bar, *söröző*. A half-litre of beer is a *korsó*.

### Restaurants

There is no shortage of eating establishments in Budapest and, at the present rate of exchange, they are good value. Be adventurous and look about you while you are wandering around. There are many cheap and cheerful cafés and restaurants in the less fashionable areas of the city centre, for example along Fő utca. The common name for restaurant is either *étterem* or *vendéglő*. Menus are usually available in an eccentric English or German (sometimes French). Hungarians tend to make the mid-day meal their main meal. Look out for early closing —Hungarians tend to eat early and you will not find it easy to order a meal after 9:00 to 9:30 P.M. While credit cards are becoming more generally acceptable, you will be surprised at the number of places which still do not accept

# FOOD AND DRINK

*Fashionable Gundel Restaurant*

them, so come with plenty of cash.

**Alabárdos**, Országház utca 2, Budapest I (tel: 1560-851). Excellent food and drink in a medieval atmosphere, but pricey. Reservations essential. Closed Sunday.

**Arany Hordó**, Tárnok utca 16, Budapest I (tel: 1561-367). This restaurant, wine cellar and beer hall, in the heart of old Buda, dates from the 15th century. Open until midnight.

**Astoria**, Múzeum körút, Budapest V. A Gösser beer bar which also sells very reasonably priced meals. Favoured by young Hungarians. Closes 11:00P.M.

**Dominican and Kalocsa Restaurants** (Hilton Hotel), Szentháromság tér, Budapest (tel: 1751-000). The Dominican specialises in international and French dishes (gooseliver a

establishments in Budapest, it takes its name from Károly Gundel, who became the owner in 1910. Formerly a favourite haunt of politicians, artists and diplomats, it is still fashionable. Hungarian cuisine, of course, and gypsy music. Closes midnight.

**Japan**, Luther utca 4–6, Budapest VIII (tel: 1143-427). Situated off Rákóczi út, this smart establishment specialises, as the name implies, in Japanese cuisine. Open noon–midnight.

**Margitkert Restaurant**, Margit utca 15, Budapest (tel: 1354-791). Located in the affluent Rózsadomb district (not far from the Margaret Bridge), the Margitkert is patronised by bingeing foreign tourists and wealthy Hungarians. The food is delicious and only moderately expensive but watch out for over-charging. Gypsy music with a western orientation. Reservations essential. Major credit cards.

**Mátyás Prince**, Március 15 tér 7, Budapest V (tel: 1181-693). Much favoured by Hungarians, this centrally situated restaurant (near the Elizabeth Bridge) is decorated with scenes from the life of King Matthias Corvinus. Gypsy music a speciality.

**Ménes Csárda**, Apáczai Csere János utca 15, Budapest V (tel: 1170-803). This excellent restaurant is situated between the Forum Hotel and Váci utca. Typical Hungarian dishes are cooked at your table to the accompaniment of a cymbalom. Prices are very reasonable but credit cards are not accepted.

**Szecsuán Restaurant**, Roosevelt tér 5, Budapest V (tel: 1172-407).

speciality), while the Kalocsa offers a Hungarian menu. Gypsy music in the latter. Closes midnight.

**Duna Korzó**, Vigadó tér 3, Budapest V (tel: 1186-362). Eat out on the terrace in the summer and you will have a fine view across the Danube to Buda. Cheap and cheerful.

**Gundel Restaurant**, Állatkerti út 2, Városliget (City Park), Budapest XIV (tel: 1221-002). One of the most famous eating

## FOOD AND DRINK

As the name implies, a Chinese restaurant, which stays open until 1:00A.M. on Friday and Saturday. Closed Sunday.
**Tabáni Kakas**, Attila út 27, Budapest I (tel: 1757-165). An intimate restaurant at the foot of Castle Hill. Evening meals only.
**Trombitás Restaurant**, Retek utca 12, Budapest II (tel: 1886-137). A chic Hungarian restaurant which stays open until 4:00A.M.

### The Danube Bend
**Aranysárkány**, Alkonrani utca la, Szentendre (tel: 26 116–70). French and Hungarian cuisine at affordable prices.
**Alabárdos**, Bajcsy-Zsilinszky utca 49, Esztergom. A garden restaurant serving lunch and evening meals at very reasonable prices.
**Sirály Étterem**, Rév utca 7 (tel: 26 28 376), Visegrád. Music is the special feature here. Traditional Hungarian food.

### Cafés and Pastry Shops
**Gerbeaud**, Vörösmarty tér 7, Budapest V (tel: 1181-311). This famous pastry shop dates from 1858 but takes its name from the Swiss, Emil Gerbeaud, who took it over in 1884. Very crowded but the cakes are delicious!
**Korona**, Dísz tér 16, Budapest I (tel: 1756-139). A pleasant place to break from a morning's sightseeing in Buda.
**Lukács**, Andrássy út (Népköztársaság útja) 70, Budapest VI (tel: 1321-371). Situated opposite the Puppet Theatre on the way to Kodály körönd, this café dates from the turn of the century, when it was founded by Sándor Lukács.

*The New York café—pre-war haunt of intellectuals. Now, it's pricey*

Specialises in pastries and ice cream.
**New York (Hungária)**, Erzsébet körút (Lenin körút) 9–11, Budapest VII (tel: 1223-849). Known as the New York before World War II, when it was frequented by artists and writers, and later as the Hungária, it is worth sampling for its historical associations, but you won't find it cheap. Open 7:00A.M.–10:00P.M. daily.
**Ruszwurm**, Szentháromság utca

7, Budapest I (tel: 1173-596). Just across the street from the Matthias Church, this renowned pastry shop has been here since 1827. Come early or be prepared to wait in line.

### Fast Food
**In and around Váci utca:**
McDonalds (entrance in Régiposta utca) is now well established but there is still a permanent line. The same may be true at the nearby City Grill. If so, there's a Pizzeria in Váci and an Expresso bar. The International Trade Centre has a number of cafés and restaurants including the Taverna Grill.

**In and around Marx tér:** The West End Shopping Center, behind the Western Station, has a number of fast food service points. You will find more on nearby Teréz körút (Lenin körút). There is a McDonalds on Marx tér.

There is also plenty of fast food on sale at the western end of Rákóczi út between Blaha Lujza, tér and the Astoria.

If you want something Hungarian, stop in at a bar or *Étterem* (restaurant).

## SHOPPING

Budapest is an extremely consumer-orientated city and far ahead, in terms of shops, of other former Eastern bloc countries. You will find a wide variety of stores: many of them organised along Western lines. The price of **food** has risen

*The covered market, Tolbuhin körút*

astronomically and supermarkets are the most accessible (and often the cheapest) places to buy food. They also offer souvenirs to take home, like Hungarian wine and tins of paprika. Fruit and vegetables, which are still relatively cheap, are sold from stalls throughout the city, but it is better to go to the nagycsarnok on Tolbuhin körút, Budapest's

main market hall. Here you will find a rich variety of fruit and vegetables and festoons of scarlet paprika strung up over the traders' stalls (open daily from 6:00A.M. except Mondays, when it opens at 9:00A.M.; closed Sundays).

Other markets are held at Bosnyák tér, Budapest XIV, Elmunkás tér, Budapest XIII (which is also open on Sunday morning) and a flea market at Nagykörösi út, Budapest XIX (open Monday to Friday 8:00A.M.–4:00P.M., Saturday 8:00A.M.–3:00P.M.), which sells just about everything in the bric-à-brac line.

**Clothes** are often cheaper than they are in the West, although the gap is narrowing all the time. The department stores (*áruház*) on Rákóczi út might render up some stylish bargains.

**Records and books** are definitely good values, and on the music scene you will find everything from classical to rock for considerably less money than you would spend at home. For records and tapes there are the *zeneművesbolt* (musical culture) or *hanglemez* (sounds) shops on Petöfi and Váci utca and Vörösmarty tér in the Belváros area of Budapest. There is also a variety of record shops on Rákóczi út.

The bookshop at Váci utca 32 is a popular one with tourists. It stocks a range of novels and coffee-table books by Hungarian authors published in foreign languages.

The best selection of **maps** can be found at 1065 Budapest Bajcsy Zsilinszky út 37 or 1072 Budapest Nyár u1. Both of these are outlets for the Cartographia company and, if you plan to travel to other former Eastern bloc countries, the maps here are better than anything available when you arrive.

**Souvenirs and Presents**

Intertourist and Konsumtourist shops accept only convertible currency but goods bought at either outlet can be taken out of the country duty free (but keep the receipts, as these must be shown to the Customs when leaving).

Intertourist sells folk art, food and drink, various souvenirs and foreign language books. The main branch of Intertourist is at Budapest V, Kigyó u5 and there are branches in all the major hotels. The main Konsumtourist store is at Budapest VI, Andrássy út (Népköstársaság útja) 27.

**What to Buy**

**Folk art** is very popular in Hungary and provides unusual and often inexpensive gifts or souvenirs of your visit. Splendid carved and engraved wooden furniture is left in its natural colour; 'tulip chests' (trousseau chests) are painted with flower designs on a blue background. Smaller items include salt cellars and kitchen implements: these are made from wood, or sometimes horn, and adorned with figures from folk tales. Aside from these there are hand-woven and hand-embroidered shirts; the beautiful embroidered patterns include the simple black and white designs of southeastern Hungary and Transdanubia Mezőkövesd. Hand-woven and embroidered

*Váci utca—fashionable shopping*

pillows, tablecloths and curtains (often seen in the parlours of local homes), coats and jackets, hand-knotted rugs and bone lace are also sold to tourists. Hungary's most famous **porcelain** is Herend china, noted for its hand-painted folk flower motifs and extremely expensive to buy in the West. But modern folk pottery, made from terracotta or the 'black' vases from Nádudvar, colourfully painted plates, dishes and jugs and bokály jug-like vessels (with no pouring lip) are equally tempting purchases.

There is a craft market on Saturdays and Sundays (9:00A.M. to 2:00P.M.) on Petőfi Csarnok, which is a good place to view and buy decorative folk art. Other shops selling folk art and crafts include those at:
V. Váci u14
V. Kossuth Lajos u2
V. Régiposta u12
VII Lenin körút 5
XIII Szent István körút 26
Judit Folklor, Országház utca 12.
**Antiques** can be a good buy in Hungary, although you won't necessarily find many bargains. You can buy antiques at Felszabadulás tér 3 (furniture,

Kóssuth Lajos utca, Rákóczi út, Múzeum körút and Andrássy út. Most **supermarkets** are known by their trade name, eg ABC, and department stores known as *aruhaz*. Other shops are often known by the names of what they sell and do not have names as we know them in the West. It is worth taking Hungarian and foreign currency with you when you shop—credit cards are not widely accepted.

Saturday is not a good day to shop: the supermarkets are crowded and many of the smaller shops are shut after 1:00P.M. One thing that Budapest does have in common with the other former Eastern bloc countries is its system of making purchases in the larger non-food stores. The procedure is to select what you want to buy; collect a bill; pay at a separate till and then return to the counter and collect the goods. VAT, charged at 25 per cent, is included in the price of most goods and services.

**Food** can be bought day and night every day at the Skálá Csarnok in Klauzál tér. See also pages 88–9.

china and paintings), Felszabadulás tér 5 (carpets) and V Kossuth Lajos ul/3 (furniture, china, pictures, etc). In the Váci utca and neighbouring streets you will find the shops of Adidas, Benetton, Estée Lauder and La Boutique Swiss. The International Trade Centre is at Helia-D Váci út 19 (sells, among other things, cosmetics). For **electrical goods** go to Saba-Revox on Párisi utca 19 6A. There is a modern precinct called Skálá Metro at Marx tér, Budapest VI and the following streets are also commercial:

### Opening hours

Department stores: Monday to Wednesday, Friday 10:00A.M.–6:00P.M., Thursday 10:00A.M.–8:00P.M. Saturday 10:00A.M. to 1:00P.M. Sunday generally closed.

Food shops: Monday to Friday 7:00A.M.–7:00P.M., Saturday 7:00A.M.–2:00P.M.

On Sundays, shops are generally closed, although it is quite easy to find milk, bread, pastries, etc from 6:00A.M. to 2:00P.M.

## ACCOMMODATION

Traditionally, because there simply has not been the demand, there has not been much hotel accommodation in Hungary. Now, however, things have changed and in Budapest alone several new hotels (marked * below) are currently being constructed. A selection is listed below. Because of the general scarcity, it is advisable to book well in advance, especially in the summer.

Book through:
Hungarian Hotels Sales Office, 1888 Century Park East, Suite 827, Century City, Los Angeles, CA 90067 (tel: (213) 448-4321)

*The Atrium Hyatt and the Forum Hotels*

IBUSZ Travel Bureau, One Parker Plaza Suite 1104, Fort Lee, N.J. 07024 (tel: (201) 592-8585)

Hungarian Air Tours (Pannonia Hotels), 3 Heddon Street, London W1R 7LE (tel: (071) 437 1622)

The Hungarian Tourist Board issues an annual list of accommodation in *Hotel–Camping*, obtainable from the IBUSZ office, 3 Petőfi tér, Budapest V. They also run a 24-hour service for booking accommodation (tel: 1184-842). The hotels are graded from 1 to 5 star. Most hotels in Budapest claim to offer luxury accommodation and service. Private rooms and some flats are also available through the booking agencies, but prices for

these vary enormously. Outside Budapest, signs offering *szoba kiadó* or *zimmer* (rooms) will be seen along major roads. You can usually get a room here without making a reservation. Cheaper accommodation takes the form of hostels with dormitory-style bedrooms. The Express, Youth Travel Service, Szabadság tér 16, Budapest V, has details of available beds. It is also possible to rent bungalows on campsites. See also **Camping** p.109, and **Student and Youth Travel** p.122.

### Hotels–Budapest

**Astoria Hotel**, Kossuth Lajos utca 19, Budapest V (tel: 1173-411, telex: 22-4205), 3-star, 129 rooms. Fine fin-de-siècle building, gentlemen's club style bar. Handy for the Metro and Váci utca.

**Atrium Hyatt Hotel**, Roosevelt tér 2, Budapest V (tel: 1383-000, telex: 22-5484), 5-star, 335 rooms. International hotel and conference centre overlooking the Danube and the picturesque Castle Hill area.

**Béke Hotel**, Teréz körút (Lenin körút) 97, Budapest VI (tel: 1323-300, telex: 22-5748), 4-star, 238 rooms. On the beltway a short Metro ride from the city centre.

**Buda Penta**, Krisztina-körút 41–3, Budapest I (tel: 1566-333) 4-star, 384 rooms. Nice situation, close to the castle.

**\*Cooptourist Hotel**, Rákóczi út, Budapest VII, 255 rooms. A Hungarian–Austrian joint venture. Close to the shopping area.

**Duna Intercontinental Hotel**, Apáczai Csere János utca 4, Budapest V (tel: 1175-122, telex:

22-5277), 5-star, 340 rooms.
Views across the Danube.
**Forum Hotel**, Apáczai Csere
János utca 12–14 Budapest V
(tel: 1178-088, telex: 22-4178),
4-star, 392 rooms. Centrally
situated with Danube views.
**Gellért Hotel**, Gellért tér 1, 1111
Budapest XI (tel: 1460-700, telex:

*The pool at the Gellért, a traditional
spa hotel*

22-4363), 4-star, 221 rooms.
Traditional spa hotel, situated at
the foot of Gellért Hill. Recently
renovated, Secessionist-style
building of early 1900s.
**Grand Hotel Hungaria**, Rákóczi

út 88–92, Budapest VII (tel: 1229-050, telex: 22-4987), 4-star, 508 rooms. A short walk from the Eastern Railway Station.

**Hilton Hotel**, Hess András tér 1–3, Budapest I (tel: 1751-000, telex: 22-5984), 5-star, 320 rooms. Building incorporates part of an abbey and a church. On a prime site in the heart of Buda.

***Kempinski Hotel**, Deák tér, Budapest V, 384 rooms, suites and 2 presidential apartments. A Hungarian–German joint venture. Built primarily for business people visiting the International Trade Centre opposite. Facilities for handicapped. Billed as 'the first super de luxe hotel of the capital'.

**Korona Hotel**, Kecskeméti utca 10–12, Budapest V (tel: 1180-999), 443 rooms. In a prime position at Kálvin tér, opposite the National Museum. A Hungarian–Austrian joint venture.

**Liget Hotel**, Dózsa György út 106, Budapest VI (tel: 1110-493), 140 rooms. Overlooking the Fine Art Museum and the Zoo in the City Park. A Hungarian–Austrian joint venture.

**Metropol Hotel**, Rákóczi út 58, Budapest VII (tel: 1421–175), 2-star, 100 rooms. Basic facilities in a busy downtown setting.

**Ramada Grand Hotel**, Margit-sziget, Budapest XIII (tel: 1111-000, telex: 22-6682), 3-star, 153 rooms. A beautiful setting on Margaret Island for this old spa hotel.

**Royal Hotel**, Erzsébet körút (Lenin körút) 49, Budapest VII (tel: 1533-133, telex: 22-4463), 4-star, 311 rooms. On the beltway, near the Western Railway Station.

**Park Hotel**, Baross tér 10,

Budapest VIII (tel: 1131-420) 2-star. Basic facilities and centrally situated, close to the Eastern Railway Station.

**Taverna Hotel**, Váci utca 20, Budapest V (tel: 1384-999, telex: 22-7294), 3-star, 224 rooms. Part of an entertainment complex at the heart of the shopping district.

**Thermal Hotel**, Margit-sziget, Budapest XIII (tel: 1321-100, telex: 22-5463), 5-star, 198 rooms. A modern spa hotel, on the Margaret Island in the middle of the Danube.

***Thermal Aquincum Hotel**, Árpádfejedelem útja, Budapest III, 584 rooms. A Hungarian–Swiss joint venture. Some rooms have views across to Margaret Island.

**Thermal Helia Hotel**, Kárpát utca 62–64, Budapest XIII (tel: 1121-000), 254 rooms and 8 suites. A Hungarian–Finnish joint venture, situated opposite the Thermal Aquincum Hotel (see above).

### Hotels—Lake Balaton

**Hotel Marina**, Széchenyi utca 26, Balatonfüred (tel: 86 43 644), 3-star, 800 beds.

**Európa Hotel**, Petőfi-sétány 15, Siófok (tel: 84 13 4 11), 3-star, 275 beds.

**Hotel Auróra**, Bajcsy-Zsilinszky utca 14, Balatonalmádi (tel: 80 38 810), 3-star, 480 beds.

### Hotels—Danube Bend

**Hotel Esztergom**, Primás sziget, Esztergom (tel: 81-68), 3-star, 70 beds.

**Hotel Danubius**, Ady Endre utca 28, Szentendre (tel: 0036–26/12511), 2-star, 75 beds.

**Hotel Szilvanus**, Feketehegy, Visegrád (tel: 26 28 311), 3-star, 160 beds.

## CULTURE, ENTERTAINMENT, NIGHTLIFE

Budapest has a lively nightlife, catering to most tastes. Although many restaurants close at 11:00P.M., you can always get a meal later in the big hotels, especially on weekends. Concerts and theatre performances usually begin at 7:30P.M. Nightclubs are on the increase and some stay open as late as 3:00 or 4:00A.M. The Metro, remember, closes down at around 11:00P.M. (but taxis are cheap by Western standards).

### Music
Musically, Budapest is as well served as any major city in the West, maintaining the strong tradition Hungary has always had of nurturing some of the world's greatest conductors, composers and performers. The city has two opera houses and three major concert halls. In the summer, the concert halls close but performances continue out of doors. You can hear grand opera or Hungarian folk music, for example, on Margaret Island's open-air stage or rock music at the Buda Youth Park. In the field of classical music, Bartók, Kodály and Liszt hold pride of place. The spring and autumn Budapest Music Weeks are highlights of the year for concert-goers, and the State Opera is widely acclaimed at home and abroad.
Tourist information centres will have *Programme in Hungary*, a monthly free publication, listing all major concerts. Look out too for wall-posters advertising special events.

### Main concert halls
Academy of Music, Liszt Ferenc tér 8, Budapest VI (tel: 1420-179). National Philharmonia (Országos Filharmónia Központi Jegyirodája), Vörösmarty tér 1, Budapest V (tel: 1176-222). Ticket office for advance reservations open Monday to Friday 11:00A.M.–2:00P.M. and 2:30–6:00P.M.

### Opera and Operetta
State Opera House, Andrássy út (Népköztársaság útja) 22, Budapest VI (tel: 1312-550). Erkel Theatre, Köztársaság tér 30, Budapest VIII (tel: 1330-540). Operetta Theatre, Nagymező utca 17, Budapest VI (tel: 1320-535).

### Musicals
(*Cats, Evita, Les Misérables* etc) are regularly performed at a number of smaller theatres. For example:
Madách, Erzsébet körút (Lenin körút) 31–3, Budapest VII. Thália, Nagymező utca 22, Budapest VI.

### Gypsy music
It varies in degrees of authenticity, but it abounds in restaurants and cafés.

### Traditional Hungarian music and dance
This can be seen on stage at the Municipal Folklore Centre, Fehérvári út 47, Budapest XI.

### Theatre
Theatre tickets (programmes in Hungarian) can be obtained from: the Central Theatre Ticket Office (Színházak Központi Jegyirodája), Andrássy út (Népköztársaság útja) 18 (tel: 1120-000), open Monday to

Friday 10:00A.M.–2:00P.M. and
2:30–7:00P.M.

## Cinema

Most foreign films are dubbed
into Hungarian, rendering them
incomprehensible to foreign
visitors.

## Nightclubs

**Casanova Piano Bar**, Batthyány
tér 4, Budapest 1 (tel: 1358-320).
Open from 10:00P.M. to 5:00A.M.
for non-stop music.
**Havanna Club** (Hotel Thermal),
Margaret Island (tel: 1111-000).
Non-stop Latin-American and
dance music, open 10:00P.M. to
3:00A.M.
**Moulin Rouge**, Nagymező utca
17, Budapest VI (tel: 1112-460).
Variety shows at 10:00P.M. and
midnight.
**Orfeum** (Hotel Béke Radisson),
Teréz körút (Lenin körút) 97,

Budapest VI (tel: 1323-300).
Elegant club where the show
starts at 10:45P.M.. Open:
9:00P.M.–4:00A.M.

## Dance Clubs

Dance clubs abound in Budapest
and new ones are opening all
the time:
**Novotel** (Thursdays), Alkotás
utca 63–7, Budapest XII (tel:
1869-588).
**Hyatt Hotel** (Fridays), Roosevelt
tér 2, Budapest V (tel: 1383-000).
Open 9:00P.M.–3:00A.M.

## Casino

**The Budapest Casino** is in the
Hilton Hotel, Hess András tér
1–3 (tel: 1868-859). Offers
roulette, baccarat, blackjack and
machines. Passports have to be

*Live music is a strong tradition in
Hungary*

shown. *Open:* 5:00 P.M. to 3:00 A.M.
**Schönbrunn Boat Casino** is at
the Pest end of the Chain Bridge
(Lánchíd). Roulette, blackjack
and video games. *Open:* April to
October, 5:00 P.M.–3:00 A.M.

## WEATHER & WHEN TO GO

Budapest is at its coldest in
January, when the average
temperature drops to 29°F
(–2°C). Spring often produces
warm spells. In July, the average
temperature rises to 72°F (22°C)
but be prepared for much hotter
weather 85°F plus (30°C). The
humidity during August,
especially in Budapest itself, can
make sightseeing unpleasant but
theatre and opera performances
are held in the open air to
compensate. Hungary boasts
over 2,000 hours of sunshine a
year and a visit during the
milder spring or autumn months
(when the Budapest festivals are
held) could be rewarding.

---

**Weather Chart Conversion**
25.4mm = 1 inch
°F = 1.8 × °C + 32

---

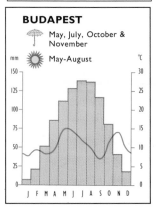

**BUDAPEST**

☂ May, July, October &
   November

☀ May–August

## HOW TO BE A LOCAL

On the face of it, a difficult
proposition given the
remoteness of the language.
German is the preferred *lingua
franca*—a reminder of Hungary's
imperial past—but nowadays
many young people have at least
a smattering of English. Try to
learn the Magyar words for good
day, please and thank you (see
**Language** below pp. 124–5).
Even a token effort will win you
friends. Wander off the beaten
track as much as possible—you
have a map, the streets are well
signposted and there is an
efficient public transportation
system, so you are not likely to
go far wrong. Drop in at a small
bar or *étterem* (restaurant) and
you will be eating and drinking
in authentic surroundings.

The **Turkish baths** are a popular
haunt for world-weary
Hungarians, anxious to catch up
on the gossip and if you are not
totally daunted by problems
posed by the language, a visit to
one of the baths is certainly
recommended. They vary greatly
—locals tend to use the cheaper
ones, tourists may prefer
something like the beautiful, but
expensive, Gellért baths (worth
a visit for the internal decor even
if you don't take the waters).
There are all sorts of specialist
treatments—cardiac, kidney,
gynaecological etc—but the
basics are a sauna (szauna),
followed by a vigorous massage
(masszázs), then a soak in the hot
pool (gőzfürdő), which is where
the locals tend to spend hours
just sitting and chatting. These
are all segregated, so make sure
you know the words for 'men'

and 'women'. You will have to throw away all inhibitions, as everyone wanders around completely naked or, at most, in a little apron provided by the establishment, and the attendants and masseuses tend to be somewhat joyless and unsmiling. After the hot pool, return to your locker to find your swimsuit and the communal pool for a swim.

## CHILDREN

Very young children are not particularly well catered to in Budapest. Only the largest hotels offer a baby-sitting service, cribs, highchairs etc. However, baby food, disposable diapers

*City Park: all the fun of the fair*

and other basics are available in most supermarkets. The situation is better where older children are concerned. Young people up to 14 years old are eligible for reductions on all public transportation and at campsites.

**Boating and cab rides:** in summer, boats can be rented on the lake in City Park. For a more expensive treat, why not try a boat trip along the Danube or a ride in a horse-drawn cab (*fiacre*) in Buda?

**City Park:** (Városliget): within its confines you will find a Zoo (Állatkert), open from 9:00 A.M. to 6:00 P.M., an Amusement Park (Vidám Park), open from 10:00 A.M. to 7:00 P.M., and a spectacular Circus (Nagycirkusz) with human and animal acts (Performances: Wednesday,

## CHILDREN

Thursday, Friday 3:00P.M. and
7:00P.M., Saturday 3:00P.M.,
Sunday 10:00A.M., 3:00P.M.
Closed Monday, Tuesday).
The **Kőzlekedési Múzeum**
(Transportation Museum) too
can be recommended.

**Picnics and playgrounds:** if the
weather is hot, you may want to
go for a picnic. There are seats,
as well as open spaces, in the
City Park, on Margaret Island
(where there is also a small
children's zoo), in the children's
playground, Szabadság tér, and
in Jubileum Park on the slopes of
Gellért Hill.

**Theatre for children:** children
will enjoy a performance by the
colourful marionettes of the State
Puppet Theatre (Állami
Bábszinház), Andrássy út
(Népköztársaság útja) 69, or the
laser theatre shows to the sound
of pop and classical music
(Planetárium, Metro: Népliget).
For performance details, check
with IBUSZ.

**Waxworks: (Budavári
Panoptikum)** the waxworks in
the caves beneath Castle Hill
(entrance in Úri utca 9)
concentrate on the more
gruesome and scandalous
episodes in Hungary's history
and are not for the squeamish
(*Open:* Tuesday to Sunday,
10:00A.M. to 6:00P.M.).

**Budai-hegység (The Buda
Hills)**, a little further afield, offer
a pleasant break from the noise
and fumes of the city. Take the
cogwheel railway from Szilágyi
Erzsébet fasor to Széchenyi.
From here you can ride on the
narrow-gauge Pioneer Railway
(Uttörővasút) which features
children as ticket collectors and
station masters. Alternatively,
the No. 22 bus from Moszkva tér
will take you to the Game
Reserve (Vadaspark). Alight at
the Fodor Szanatórium stop.
There is a marked nature trail
here of about three miles (5km)
(*Open:* daily 9:00A.M. to 5:00P.M.).
**The Lake Balaton resorts**
organise children's events. Ask
at the IBUSZ offices there.

## TIGHT BUDGET

### Transportation

Public transportation is very
cheap and efficient and can be
recommended as the most cost-
effective way to see Hungary.
Hitch-hiking is legal except on
turnpikes and is becoming more
common. Bicycling is prohibited
on turnpikes and on major

*Dolls in traditional folk costume*

roads (those with single digit
numbers), effectively cutting out
most routes into Budapest.
However, bikes may be taken
on to trains and some stations
even rent them out.
For further information contact
MÁV, Andrássy út
(Népköztársaság útja) 35,

Budapest VI (tel: 1228-049).
The office of the Hungarian
Cycling Federation is at
Millenáris Sporttelep, Szabó
János utca 3, Budapest IV. They
will assist with route planning.
Maps can also be obtained from
the Hungarian Camping and
Caravaning Club, Üllői út 6,
Budapest VIII (tel: 133-6536 or
114-1880).

### Accommodation
Most of the tourist offices will
arrange private accommodation,
either when you get to Budapest
or prior to leaving. This kind of
accommodation can be a real
money saver (although if you're
on your own you will almost
certainly have to pay for a
double room). The tourist offices
vet the hosts and the premises
but it would be wise to do some
research on the location you
would like to stay in and ask for a
place here. The bonus of this
type of accommodation is clearly
the chance to see the 'real'
Budapest and meet the Pestians.
It is worth trying to speak a little
Hungarian to break the ice. You
will normally be given the keys
to the apartment and may come
and go as you please.
● If you don't book through a
tourist office you can go to your
chosen location and look for
signs saying *Zimmer Frei* outside
houses and apartments; this
indicates bed and breakfast type
accommodation is available.
● If there is a group of you it is
worthwhile enquiring about
apartments to rent; do this
through your local tourist agency
before you leave for Hungary.
The cheaper hotels in Budapest
include:

**Citadella**, XI, Gellérthegy (tel:
1665-794)
**Express**, XII, Beethoven u7/8
(tel: 1753-082)
**Lidó**, III, Nánási u67 (tel:
1886-865)

## SPECIAL EVENTS

The following list covers just a
few highlights. For further
guidance, see the monthly
*Programme in Hungary*.
**February:** Film festival.
Hungarian and foreign films.
**March:** Budapest Spring Festival.

Ten days of music of all kinds plus plays, ballet, children's events, exhibitions etc. (Events now also held in Szentendre.)
**1 May:** Old-style Communist celebrations have now been abolished but the holiday is likely to remain.
International Spring Fair (concerts, folklore programmes).
**Final week of May**—book fair. Swimming season, Lake Balaton, begins with a regatta.
**20 August:** Constitution Day. Danube regatta and firework display on Gellérthegy.

*Street vendors plying their trade on one of the tourist beats*

**Late September to October:**
Budapest Arts Weeks. Concerts, theatre, ballet, film performances, art exhibitions.

## SPORTS

For details of sporting fixtures see *Programme in Hungary*.

### Angling
Fishing permits are issued from regional tourist offices or from hotel reception. A permit valid

## SPORTS

for the entire country can be obtained (with hard currency only) from the Hungarian Angling Association (MOHOSZ), Október 6 utca 20, Budapest V (tel: 1325-315).

### Horse Racing

Trotting races are held at Kerepesi út 9–11, Budapest VIII (meetings on Wednesday, Thursday, Saturday and Sunday afternoons). Flat racing, recently reintroduced, takes place at Dobi István út 2, Budapest X (Metro Örs vezér tere, then bus 100). Thursday and Sunday.

### Horse Riding

Whether you want a short ride or a week-long trek there are plenty of opportunities in the countryside around Budapest. Ask IBUSZ for details. Pegazus Tours, Károlyi Mihály utca 5, Budapest V (tel: 1171-562) also has information on tours, stables and accommodation.

### Soccer

The national team plays at the Népstadion (Metro line 2). The most popular club side is Ferencváros, named after Budapest's ninth district. League matches are usually on Saturdays, occasionally on Sundays. No games are played in January.

### Skating

The artificial lake in the City Park is frozen over for skating in winter.

### Swimming

The thermal baths can be enjoyed by the healthy as well as the sick. However, be sure to check with IBUSZ about opening times as many establishments

(the Király baths, for example) have special days for men and women only. For a list of baths, see p. 114. See also **How To Be A Local**, pp. 98–9.

The Alfréd Hajós Sport Swimming Pool on Margaret Island is the place to go for an ordinary indoor swim. Or, if the weather is good, there are open air pools at:

Szabadságpart (Freedom beach), Dagály utca, Budapest XIII.

Széchenyi baths (Vidám Park), open daily 6:00 A.M.–6:00 P.M.

Lake Balaton has a great many free beaches with swimming areas marked by buoys, also swimming pools.

There are still very few nudist beaches in Hungary. For details you should contact Naturisták Szövetsége, Kárpát utca 8, Budapest III.

### Tennis

Courts can be rented at the Tennis Stadium on Margaret Island (or arrange through IBUSZ).

### Water Sports

Motor boats are banned on Lake Balaton which makes it ideal for windsurfing. Lake Balaton, some 62 miles (100km) southwest of Budapest, is the largest lake in Central and Western Europe and can be reached from Budapest by the M 7 turnpike or by train, from the Southern Railway Station, to all the major places on its shores.

Equipment can be rented from campsites and the major beaches.

For sailing boats, contact Balatontourist Veszprém, Münnich Ferenc tér 3.

## DIRECTORY

### Contents

*Dramatically sited on the Danube, Visegrád is just two hours away*

## DIRECTORY

### Arriving

To enter Hungary you need a passport valid for at least nine months. Visas are no longer required for citizens of the United States, Canada or the United Kingdom.

Australian citizens should apply for a visa from the following address: Hungarian Consulate, Unit 6, 351a Edgecliff Road NSW 2027, Sydney (tel: (02) 328 7859). Visas (single, multiple entry and transit) can also be obtained at road border crossings and at airports but not at rail crossings. Independent visitors staying more than one month must register at a police station within 48 hours of arrival. Registration is automatic for guests at hotels, motels, campsites etc. Keep your travel documents with you at all times; report any loss to your embassy who will provide you with an exit permit and certificate which you must take to your embassy or consulate.

The national carrier is MALÉV Airlines. There are offices at the following addresses:
Rockefeller Centre,
630 Fifth Avenue, Suite 1900
New York 10111
(tel: 212 757 6480)
175 Bloor Street East,
Suite 172, Toronto, Canada
(tel: 416 944 0093)
10 Vigo Street, London W1X 1AJ
(tel: (071) 439 0577)

### By air

MALÉV and Pan Am now offer a new, twice-weekly, airbus service direct from New York to Budapest, which then returns to New York after a brief stop-over in Vienna. KLM (Royal Dutch Airlines) also flies from several centres in the US to Budapest, via Amsterdam. There are scheduled daily flights to Hungary from all European capitals and other major cities, operated by MALÉV and other national airlines. There are normally two flights per day between London and Budapest (flying time 2hrs 10mins) operated by MALÉV and British Airways. Try the following for cheaper flights/special deals in the US: Hungaria Travel Bureau, 1603 2nd Avenue, New York (tel: (212) 249 9342).

In the UK: Hungarian Air Tours, 3 Heddon Street, London W1R 7LE (tel: (071) 437 9405); Danube Travel, 6 Conduit Street, London W1R 9TG (tel: (071) 493 0263). Budapest Ferihegy airport is situated about 12 miles (20km) southeast of the city centre and has two terminals. MALÉV and Lufthansa flights land at the more modern Terminal 2. Other foreign airlines land at Terminal 1. Passport formalities are generally completed in a few minutes and the standard red/green channels are in operation for customs. The usual services such as currency exchange, hotel service, car rental and duty free are available (NB only hard currency is acceptable for the purchase of duty free items). A regular airport bus (Volán) operates from both terminals to Erzsébet tér (Engels tér) from 5:00A.M. to 11:00P.M. and takes about 40 minutes. Buy your ticket on board. Taxis are also on hand outside the airport terminal. All taxis should have meters but agree the fare beforehand. NB Taxi drivers are not permitted to demand hard

*On the Danube*

currency in payment. For more information, ask at the IBUSZ desk.

### By train
Only economical if you are under 26; otherwise the cost exceeds either air or coach travel. (For under 26s see **Student and Youth Travel** below.) There is a daily connection to Budapest from London Victoria which makes the journey in approximately 28 hours via Dover, Oostende and Vienna. Alternatively you can change in Paris and travel on the *Orient Express* (this is not incidentally, the glamorous one). All seats, sleepers or couchettes need to be booked well in advance.
If you are already in Eastern Europe there are regular services to Budapest from Vienna and Prague which connect with a number of other centres. During the summer, Saxonia Express operates a road-rail service between Dresden and Budapest carrying private cars and trailers.
NB Tourists who do need a visa, should remember that they cannot get one at the border when arriving by train.

### By boat
A reasonably priced hydrofoil service operates between Vienna and Budapest from April to October. The journey takes about five hours. The International Boat Station (MAHART) is at 1056 Belgrád rakpart. Reserve your seats here (tel: 1181-704) or through any IBUSZ office. Alternatively, seats may be reserved in Vienna at the IBUSZ office at Kartnerstrasse 26, Wien 1. Visitors may also enter by private boat, providing of course they hold a valid passport and visa where necessary.

### By bus
Regular bus services operate from Austria to various

## DIRECTORY

destinations in Hungary, including Budapest and Lake Balaton. An alternative route during the summer is via Munich in Germany. International buses arrive at Erzsébet tér (Engels tér).

*A smile never needs translation*

### By car

You can enter Hungary from approximately 30 crossing points in Austria, Czechoslovakia, Romania, the Ukraine (formerly USSR) and Yugoslavia. The main Vienna–Budapest road (E60) crosses the Hungarian border at Hegyeshalom.

## Camping

There are plenty of campsites in Hungary, many around Lake Balaton (approximately 62 miles (100km) southwest of Budapest). They are open between May and September and are graded to international standards. A basic camp includes running water, toilets, First Aid facilities, and stoves for cooking. The more elaborate include restaurants, shops, even nightclubs.

Most campsites offer reduced rates for children aged 2–14 and some sites have reductions for members of the International Camping and Caravanning Club. Bungalows can also be found on the major campsites. They sleep 2–4 people and are good value for families.

Information about campsites and their facilities can be obtained from: The Hungarian Camping and Caravanning Club (Magyar Camping és Caravaning Club), Üllői út 6, Budapest VIII (tel: 1336-536).

## Camping sites in the Budapest area (selection)

**Expo Autokemping**, X (part of the fair and exhibition area), Dobi István út 10 (Gate 4), 500 places for tourists, open mid-June–mid-September.

**Caraván**, Konkoly u18b, open April–September

**Hárs-hegy**, II (northwest edge of the city), 320 places, open Easter–October.

**Mtro-Saturnus Tenisz Kemping**, XVI (in eastern part of the city), Csömöri u158, 50 places, open April–October.

**Mini**, III (in north), Vöröshadsereg utja, 40 places, open May–September.

**Római fürdő**, III (northern edge of the city), Szentendrei út 169, 1,000 places, open all the year round.

**Tündérhegy**, XII (Buda Hills), Szilassy u8, 20 places, open all the year round.

**Zugligeti**, XII (near the chairlift at Széchenyi hegy, Buda Hills), Zugligeti út 101, 100 places, open April–mid-October.

## Camping site in Esztergom

**Vadvirág Kemping**, 500 places, open May–September.

## Camping site in Szentendre

**Kemping Papsziget**, 250 places, open May–October.

## Camping site by Lake Velence

**Panoráma Kemping**, 800 places, open mid-April–mid-October.

## Camping sites by Lake Balaton

**Kristof Kemping**, 40 places, open May–September.

**Mini Kemping**, 240 places, open May–October.

## Crime

As in many other East European countries there has been an increase in pick-pocketing and purse snatching, especially in busy shopping streets and other tourist areas. Take basic precautions to protect your property, such as locking your car, storing valuables in the hotel safe etc. Report any serious loss (documents etc) to your embassy immediately. Otherwise contact any IBUSZ representative. The Central Police Station has a thefts office at Deák Ferenc u16–18, Budapest V, but there is no guarantee that you will find an English speaker.

## DIRECTORY

**Customs Regulations**

Because of recent changes in the political situation, these are subject to change. For the latest regulations, consult a Hungarian Consulate or tourist office.

The following can be taken into Hungary duty free: 2 litres of wine, 1 litre of spirits, 250 cigarettes or 50 cigars or 250 grammes of tobacco and small presents up to a total value of approximately 5,000 forints. You are allowed to take only a maximum of 100 forints per person into Hungary but there is no limit on Western currency.

A special permit is required for a hunting rifle and for sophisticated electronic equipment.

You may not bring in: pornography of any kind, narcotics, explosives, firearms and ammunition, pure alcohol. The authorities have now relaxed their interpretation of what constitutes subversive literature, but don't push your luck!

The following can be taken out duty free: 2 litres of wine, 1 litre of spirits, 250 cigarettes or 50 cigars or 250 grammes of tobacco and small gifts. Everything else is subject to duty. Permits are not required for items bought in hard currency stores, but you must keep your receipts.

You may not enter or leave the country with surplus petrol or other fuel. A certificate is required to take plants and animals out of the country. There are certain items that you are not allowed to take out without a permit. For further guidance telephone 1326-943, or call in at Szent István tér 11B, Budapest V. *Open:* Monday to Thursday 8:00A.M.–5:00P.M., Friday 8:00A.M.–4:00P.M. See also **Money Matters**.

**Disabled People**

At present there is little special provision in Hungary for the disabled, but visitors can contact the following for advice and information:

**National Federation of the Associations of Disabled Persons**, 1032 Budapest, San Marco u76, Hungary (tel: 1888-951)

**Hungarian Society for the Rehabilitation of Disabled Persons**, PO Box 1, H 1528, Budapest 123, Hungary 1.

**Pikniktours Travel Agency** arranges tours for physically disabled people travelling within Hungary. For more information write to the Director, H-1028 Budapest, Pinceszer u14–16, Hungary.

Of the half-dozen new hotels in Budapest at least one (Kempenski, Deák tér) will have suitable rooms for receiving handicapped guests and several other hotels (eg the Thermal Hotel, Margit-sziget) have wheelchair access. Contact your tourist office to check details. Public places are generally rather poor as regards wheechair access.

**Driving**

A valid state driver's licence is sufficient although it is advisable to take an International Driving Licence; registration documents and proof of third-party insurance should also be taken.

*Public transportation is cheap and good*

All main roads in Hungary are generally good and signs follow the standard Continental system. Tickets for turnpikes, valid for three months, can be bought at border crossing points. Traffic drives on the right and trams always have the right of way. In Budapest itself, driving is as difficult as in any European capital and parking can be a nightmare, with parking spaces in short supply. The public transportation system is highly recommended here.

**Accidents** Report all accidents to the police immediately (tel: 07).

**Breakdown assistance** Contact the Hungarian Automobile Association: Francia út 38,

## DIRECTORY

Budapest XIV (tel: 1693-714, round the clock). Hungarian AA Information Centre with foreign language service, 8:00 A.M.– 4:30 P.M. Monday to Friday (tel: 1353-101). Or contact ÚTINFORM (Highway Information Centre) Dob u75, Budapest VII, (tel: 1227-052). Insurance claims should be made immediately: Hungaria International Vehicle Insurance Office, Gvadányi utca 69, Budapest XIV (tel: 1633-079, 1836-527).

**Car rental** Available in Budapest and some larger towns. You will be expected to pay in hard currency. The choice of cars is not as wide as in the West and automatic gearboxes are rare. The driver must be 21 or over and have been in possession of a licence for at least a year. The price includes comprehensive insurance coverage and motor oil.

AVIS, via IBUSZ, Martinelli tér 8, Budapest V (tel: 1184-158), and at Ferihegy airport (tel: 1475-754)

Budget, via Cooptourist, Kossuth tér 13–15, Budapest V (tel: 1131-466)

Europcar, via Volántourist, Vaskapu utca 16, Budapest IX (tel: 1334-783), and at Ferihegy airport (tel: 1342-540)

Hertz, via Főtaxi, Kertész utca 24–28 (tel: 1221-471)

**Fuel** ÁFOR petrol stations can be found along most roads. Also, around Budapest there are AGIP, BP and Shell stations (which also sell Western-made accessories). Self-service is forbidden and the attendant will expect you to round up the gas cost by way of a tip.

A few garages have lead-free

gas: the ÁFOR garage on the M7 turnpike at Budaörs, and in Budapest at Kerepesi út 5–7, district VIII and Szabadság tér, Budapest V.

**Legal requirements** Seat belts must be worn in the front seats and children under six must sit in the back. Horns should not be sounded in built-up areas. Motor cyclists must wear helmets and use dipped headlights day and night. You must carry a spare set of bulbs, a first-aid kit and a red, warning triangle to display in case of breakdown. *There is a total alcohol ban* and visitors are prosecuted with the same severity as residents.

*Folk costumes vary, but are always colourful—and worn with pride*

**Speed limit** 120kmh (75mph) on turnpikes 80kmh (50mph) for motorbikes), 100kmh (62mph) on highways 70kmh for (43mph) motorbikes), 80kmh (50mph) on main roads and 60kmh (37mph) in built-up areas 50kmh (31mph) for motorbikes).

### Electricity

The electricity supply in Hungary is at 220 volts, 50 cycles AC. Continental-sized round two-pin plugs are used. US appliances will require an adaptor, as will 13-amp, square-pin plugs.

### Embassies and Consulates

**In Budapest**
**US**, Szabadság tér 12, Budapest V (tel: 1126-450)

**Canada**, Budakeszi út 32, Budapest II (tel: 1767-711)
**Great Britain**, Harmincad utca 6, Budapest V (tel: 1182-888)
**Australia**, Délibáb utca 30, Budapest VI (tel: 1534-233)

### Hungarian Embassies and Consulates Abroad

**US** Main Consulate, 8 East 75th Street, New York NY 10021 (tel: (212) 879-4127)
**Canada** Hungarian Embassy, 7 Delaware Avenue, Ottowa K2P OZ2, Ontario (tel: (1613) 232-1549)
**Great Britain** Hungarian Consulate, 35b Eaton Place SW1 (tel: (071) 235-2664)
**Australia** Hungarian Consulate, Unit 6, 351a Edgecliff Road, NSW 2027, Sydney (tel: (02) 328-7859)

### Emergency Telephone Numbers

Ambulance 04
Fire 05
Police 07

### Entertainment Information

Tourist information centres will have *Programme in Hungary*, a monthly free publication, listing all major concerts from classical to rock. Look out for wall-posters advertising events too.
Theatre tickets can be obtained from: the Central Theatre Ticket Office (Színházak Központi Jegyirodája), Andrássy út (Népköztársaság útja) 18, (tel: 1120-000). *Open:* Monday to Friday 10:00A.M.–2:00P.M. and 2:30–7:00P.M.

### Entry formalities See Arriving

### Health Regulations

No vaccinations are necessary. The tap water is safe to drink. All visitors to Hungary receive free first aid and transportation to the hospital. However, there is a charge for all other treatment, so it is essential to take out good health insurance.

Most private clinics have at least one English-speaking doctor; many speak German. Emergency dental treatment is available at the **Institute of Stomatology**, Mária u52, Budapest VIII (tel: 1330-189). Simple medicines such as headache remedies are available without prescription but most other types of medicine require one; if you use contact lenses take any supplies of fluid, etc, with you, as these are scarce in Budapest.

**Health Care**

Emergency ambulance – tel: 04 Emergency Dentist – Dental Clinic VIII, Mária utca 52, Budapest VIII (tel: 1330-189) Hungary has the richest mineral springs in Europe. In Budapest alone, 128 thermal springs service 32 thermal baths, of which nine are officially recognised as spas. People with heart problems or high blood pressure should take medical advice before undertaking treatment in hot springs. (The Balatonfüred at Lake Balaton is recommended for those with heart disease because the water contains carbonic acid.) A selection of Budapest spas is listed below.

**Gellért**, Kelenhegyi út 4, Budapest XI. Various baths, a sauna, solarium and gym etc. The radioactive waters here can cure muscular, nervous and heart diseases.

*Open:* Monday to Friday 6:30A.M.–7:00P.M.; Saturday and Sunday 6:30A.M.–noon; wave bath (open air) and other treatments daily 6:00A.M.–7:00P.M.

**Király Fürdő** Fő utca 84, Budapest II. Original 16th-century Turkish pool with modern facilities. Open alternate days for men and women. Institute for Balneotherapy here offers treatment for rheumatism and arthritis.

*Open:* Monday to Saturday 6:30A.M.–7:00P.M.

**Rác Fürdő** Hadnagy utca 8–10, Budapest I. Spring water at 104°F (40°C) is good for the skin and for nervous disorders. Original Turkish octagonal pool with dome.

*Open:* Monday to Saturday 6:30A.M.–7:00P.M.

**Rudas Fürdő** Döbrentei tér 9, Budapest I. Built by Ali and Sokoli Mustapha, 16th-century Pashas of Buda. Recommended for kidney stones and stomach problems.

*Open:* Monday to Friday 6:30A.M.–8:00P.M., Saturday and Sunday 6:00A.M.–noon; wave bath Monday to Friday 6:00A.M.–6:00P.M., Saturday 6:00A.M.–8:00P.M., Sunday 6:00A.M.–noon.

**Széchenyi Spa**, Vidám Park, Állatkerti körút 11, Budapest XIV. Water at 76°F (26°C) effective for rheumatism and neuralgia. Undergoing renovation.

*Open:* Monday to Saturday 6:30A.M.–7:00P.M., Sunday 6:30A.M.–noon.

The private **Pető Institute,**
Kútvölgyi út 6, Budapest XII is
world-famous for its treatment of
children with spina bifida,
cerebral palsy and multiple
sclerosis.

### Holidays – Public and Religious
New Year's Day
15 March (Anniversary of 1848
Revolution)
Easter Monday
1 May (Labour Day)
20 August (Constitution Day)
Christmas Day
Boxing Day

### Lost Property
**Budapest Lost and Found** (Talált
Tárgyak Központi Hivatala),
Erzsébet tér (Engels tér) 5,
Budapest V (tel: 1174-961)
*Open:* Monday to Thursday
8:00A.M.–5:00P.M., Friday
8:00A.M.–3:00P.M.

**On public Transportation** BKV,
Akácfa utca 18, Budapest VII (tel:
1226-613)

*Open:* Monday, Tuesday,
Thursday 7:00A.M.–3:30P.M.,
Wednesday 7:00A.M.–6:00P.M.,
Friday 7:00A.M.–3:00P.M.
**For items left on trains** try also
the information offices at the
terminus stations.
**For items left on boats** contact
MAHART, Belgrád rakpart Boat
Station, Budapest V (tel:
1181-704).

### Media
Some Western newspapers and
magazines are available at the
central news-stands and in the
hotels.
*The Hungarian Times* is
published in English. The free
magazine, *Coming Events in
Hungary,* is also produced in
English and is published
monthly.
The TV Channel 2 broadcasts
bulletins for foreigners and

*Oblivious to the piece of history
commemorated in the plaque, this
resident enjoys today's news*

## DIRECTORY

occasionally has English language plays or films. Daily news in English, German and Russian is broadcast on the Petöfi radio station (VHF 66.62 MHz) at noon.

Satellite TV is available in the hotels.

### Money Matters

The unit of currency in Hungary is the forint. 1 forint = 100 fillers (you will not come across this smaller unit often). A maximum of 100 forints can be taken in or out of the country. When you leave you are allowed to exchange up to half your remaining forints to a maximum value of $100, so keep all receipts. A single official exchange rate for the forint is set daily by the Hungarian National Bank. Money can be exchanged at any of the following: branches of the National Bank and of the savings bank OTP, travel agencies, hotels, most campsites and some border posts. Travellers' cheques and, sometimes, Eurocheques are acceptable as well as cash. Hungarian banks do not open on weekends and many tourist offices close at 4:00 P.M. during the week. Take your passport for identification.

It is inevitable that some time during your stay in Hungary you will be approached by individuals offering to change money on the black market. This practice is illegal and you are advised to ignore any such offers, no matter how tempting, especially as rubbish paper is often wedged between real notes. (In fact, these unofficial rates are often unattractive.)

International credit cards can be used instead of cash in some large restaurants, hotels and shops.

Note that hard currency is virtually impossible to obtain at the moment (it is simply too vital to the national economy to be dispensed back to foreigners). In dire emergencies only, contact your embassy or consulate. Lost travellers' cheques should be reported immediately to the Hungarian National Bank, Szabadság tér 8/9, Budapest V (tel: 1123-223). *Open:* Monday to Friday 9:00 A.M. to 1:00 P.M.

### Opening Times

**Banks** Monday to Friday 9:00 A.M.–5:00 P.M., Saturday 9:00 A.M.–2:00 P.M.

**Food shops** Monday to Friday 6:00 or 7:00 A.M. to 7:00 or 8:00 P.M., Saturday 10:00 A.M.–2:00 P.M.

**Museums** Generally, Tuesday to Sunday 10:00 A.M.–6:00 P.M. Times, however, will vary, especially in the smaller museums. Check at your hotel information desk.

**Offices** Generally Monday to Friday 8:30 A.M.–5:30 P.M.

**Post Offices** Monday to Friday 8:00 A.M.–6:00 P.M., Saturday 8:00 A.M.–2:00 P.M. There are two 24-hour/seven-day post offices in Budapest: at Teréz körút (Lenin körút) 105 and Baross tér.

**Stores** Monday to Friday 9:00 or 10:00 A.M.–6:00 or 7:00 P.M., (Thursday till 8:00 P.M.), Saturday 10:00 A.M.–2:00 P.M.

### Personal Safety

Theft is on the increase in Hungary as tourism expands, so watch your wallet or purse, especially in crowds. As in any

*Village Museum church, Szentendre*

city, women may suffer sexual harassment when travelling alone, although Budapest is certainly not among the worst European cities in this respect. Avoid travelling on the 'black train' which leaves Budapest on Friday nights for Debrecen – it is notorious for carrying drunken, brawling migrant workers. Dial 07 for emergencies.

**Pharmacies** (Gyógyszertár or Patika)
*Open:* Monday to Friday 8:00A.M.–8:00P.M., Saturdays 8:00A.M.–2:00P.M.
Illuminated signs in the windows give addresses of the nearest 24hr pharmacies.
Pharmacies issue a wide range of drugs, but mostly of East European origin. If, therefore, you require special medication, take it with you. In all pharmacies, you will be expected to place your order,

then pay at the cash register before returning to the counter to collect your items.

### 24-hour seven-day pharmacies in Budapest
Alkotás utca 1b, Budapest XII (tel: 1554-691)
Rákóczi út 86, Budapest VII (tel: 1229-613)
Széna tér 1, Budapest I (tel: 1353-704)
Teréz körút (Lenin körút) 95, Budapest VI (tel: 1114-439)

### Places of Worship
The majority of Hungarians are Roman Catholics but there are also Protestant, Eastern Orthodox and Jewish minorities. Most large churches are open throughout the day but the smaller ones usually open only at service times.
Visitors are expected to wear modest dress and to refrain from sightseeing while services are in progress.
Mass is held in Hungarian at the

## DIRECTORY

Mátyás-templom (Matthias Church) in Buda. Jewish Synagogue, Dohány utca 2, Budapest VII: from April to September there are services on Saturdays at 10:00A.M.

### Church services in English are held at

Evangelical Budavari Church, Táncsics Mihály utca 28, Budapest I: services on Sundays at 10:30A.M.

Scottish Mission Church, No.51

*The Basilica, Esztergom*

Vörösmarty utca, Budapest VI: services every Sunday at 11:15A.M.

Catholic Church of Christ the King, No. 9 Reviczky utca, Budapest VIII: services on the last Sunday of the month at 11:15A.M.

Catholic Church of St Elizabeth, Rószák tere 8, Budapest VII: services on the second Sunday of the month at 5:00P.M.

### Police

Most police officers have a smattering of German but no

other languages. However, they have a good reputation for being helpful to tourists. Their uniforms are blue and grey. Traffic police are distinguished by white caps and white leather accessories. Police cars are blue and white. The central Police Station in Budapest is at Deák Ferenc u16–18, Budapest V (tel: 118-0800). Advice for foreign tourists tel: 111-8668.

### Post Office

*Open:* Monday to Friday 8:00A.M.–6:00P.M., Saturday 8:00A.M.–2:00P.M.

There are 24-hour, seven-day post offices near the Western and Eastern Railway Stations (Teréz körút (Lenin körút) 105 and Baross tér 11c respectively). Post restante mail can be collected from Post Office No. 4, Városház utca 18. Remember that Hungarians put surnames first so your letters may be filed under your first name initial by mistake.

Stamps can also be bought at tobacconists (*bélyeg*) and in hotels. Mailboxes, which are emptied daily, are red and decorated with a hunting horn. For Telegrams, dial 02 (occasionally an English-speaking operator can be found) or stop at a main post office. Telex machines can be found in most hotels and at the Central Telecommunications Post Office at Petőfi Sándor utca 13–19, Budapest V.

### Public Transportation

**Boats** Boats services operate along the Danube and on Lake Balaton from April to late September. The MAHART service between Budapest and the towns on the Danube bend leaves from Vigadó tér boat station (tel: 1181-223). Vienna can be reached by a hydrofoil service which leaves from the International Boat Station on Belgrád rakpart. For reservations contact an IBUSZ office or MAHART, Belgrád rakpart (tel: 1181-704).

**Buses** (Say 'booss' for bus, not 'bus', which is rude in Hungarian!) Buses are cheap but crowded, especially at rush hours. Timetables are available at the main bus terminal, Erzsébet tér (Engels tér), but in the heavy city traffic don't rely on the schedules. There are some night buses, but most services end at 11:00P.M. Bus stops display a blue-bordered bus symbol and the letter 'M'; there is usually a route map and a list of stops. Blue bus tickets (which must be purchased in advance) can be bought from machines, metro stations and tobacco shops – one ticket per ride. They should be validated as you board. Bus and tram tickets are not interchangeable. Long distance buses run to other towns and resorts. Seats must be reserved in advance. For further information contact Erzsébet tér (Engels tér) Bus Station. International services operate to Vienna, Munich and Venice. Buy tickets in hard currency.

**Metro** Budapest's underground system was the first to be built on mainland Europe and was opened in 1896 for the millennial celebrations. There are now three lines (blue No. 3, red No. 2 and yellow No. 1) intersecting at Deák tér. The system is fast, clean and safe. Routes are

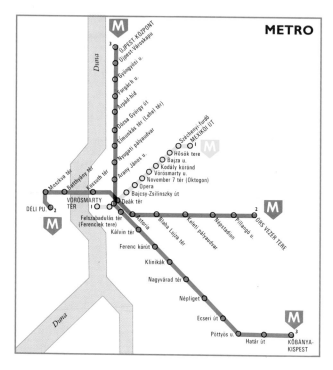

clearly indicated and all stations display maps. Trains operate from 4:30A.M. to 11:00P.M., so beware of missing last connections!

There is a flat fare for each journey. Buy a yellow ticket from the machine in the entrance or from the ticket window, then punch it in the machine as you approach the escalator. (On the yellow line, the tickets have to be punched on the train.) A new ticket is needed if you change lines.

**Taxis** Budapest taxis are cheap and plentiful. All cabs are fitted with meters and charges are usually displayed. Pay only in

forints but add a 10 per cent tip. Cabs may be hired from a stand, hailed, or ordered by phone, but do not expect the drivers to speak a foreign language.
Tel: Buda Taxi 1294-000;
Főtaxi 1222-222;
City Taxi 1228-855;
Radio Taxi 1271-271.

**Trains** Hungary has a cheap and efficient rail network and all the main provincal towns can be reached by express train from Budapest (seat reservations essential). The HÉV suburban railway serves Budapest and its environs. Yellow signs indicate departures (*induló*), white ones arrivals (*érkező*). Tickets (also yellow) may be used for stations within the city limits. Other tickets can be bought up to 60 days in advance and various concessions are available: children under 4 travel free; those aged 4–10 travel at half price and there are reduced rates for groups and senior citizens. Seven and ten-day excursion tickets are also available. For tickets and information contact the MÁV Central Booking Office, Andrássy út (Népköztársaság útja) 35, Budapest VI. Tel: 1228-056 or 1228-049 for an English language information service during office hours. Most international trains leave from the East Station (Keleti pu). All international fares must be paid in hard currency.

**Trams and trolley-buses**

Services operate between 5:00A.M. and 11:00P.M. (There is a limited night service.) Tickets (yellow) are sold at metro stations, tobacconists, kiosks and by vending machines – punch them as you board.

*Budapest's Central Market Hall, built in the 1890s*

You can also buy a 24-hour ticket (*napijegy*) which enables you to travel by bus, tram, metro and suburban train (HÉV) anywhere in the city. Monthly season tickets are also available.

## Senior Citizens

Senior citizens with Rail Europe Senior Cards can claim a 33 per cent reduction on train fares in Hungary.

## Student and Youth Travel

An International Union of Students card (the East European equivalent of ISIC) will entitle you to reductions at hostels and campsites, reduced admission to museums, and generous discounts on trains and MALÉV flights. The Youth Express Travel Office, Szabadság tér 16, Budapest V (tel: 1317-777) provides information on all student discounts and opportunities in Hungary. They will also help with hostel accommodation. IUS, International Student Identity and International Youth Hostel Federation cards can all be bought here but take a plentiful supply of passport-sized photographs with you. See also **Camping** p.109 and **Accommodation** pp.92–3 and 102. There are few facilities for bicyclists in Hungary. It is illegal to bicycle on turnpikes and major main roads but some

*Public telephone kiosk*

stations have bikes for rent.
The Hungarian Cycling
Federation Office is at Millenáris
Sporttelep, Szabó János utca 3,
Budapest IV.

## Telephones

Most phone booths are green-
and-yellow or white. For long-
distance calls inside Hungary
dial 06, the district code, then
the individual number.
English language directory
enquiries (7:00A.M.–8:00P.M.) tel:
1172-200.
Use the red telephone kiosks to
make international calls. If you
get into difficulties dial the
international operator on 09.
For international calls dial 00,
before the country code, area
code and number:
United States 00-1
Canada 00-1
Britain 00-44
Australia 00-61
New Zealand 00-64
When phoning into Hungary
from abroad, the country code is
36 and the Budapest code is 1.

## Time

Central European time is six
hours ahead of the United States
(Eastern Seaboard Time) and
Canada.

## Tipping

Tipping is customary in
Hungary. Porters, maids,
cloakroom attendants, guides,
garage attendants, waiters and,
of course, gypsy violinists will all
expect tips of between 20 and
100 forints.
There are no hard and fast rules
but 10–15 per cent is standard
for waiters and taxi drivers.
The custom is to tip at the same
time as paying.

## Toilets

There are plenty of public toilets
in Budapest. As elsewhere those
in cafés, restaurants or hotels
tend to be cleaner. Leave a few
forints in the saucer by the door.
**Signs** *mosdó* or *WC: férfi*–men,
*nöi*–women

## Tourist Offices

### In Hungary

Tourinform, Sütő utca 2,
Budapest (near Deák tér) (tel:
1179-800)
Balatontourist, Blaha Lujza utca
5, Balatonfüred (tel: 86 42 822)
Dunatours, Bogdányi utca 1,
Szentendre (tel: 86 43 435)
Siotour, Szabadság tér 6, Siófok
(tel: 84 10 900)

### In United States

IBUSZ One Parker Plaza, Suite
1104, Fort Lee, N.J. 07024 (tel:
201 592 8585)

### In Great Britain

Danube Travel Ltd (IBUSZ), 6
Conduit Street, London W1R
9TG (tel: (071) 493-0263)

## Travel Agencies

### In Hungary

IBUSZ, Felszabadulás tér 5,
Budapest V (tel: 1186-866)
IBUSZ Hotel Service, Petőfi tér 3,
Budapest V (tel: 1185-707)
Budapest Tourist, Roosevelt tér
5–7 (tel: 1173-555)
Express Youth Travel,
Szabadság tér 17, Budapest V
(tel: 1317-777)
MAHART boat trips, Siótour,
Batthyány utca 2b, Siófok (tel: 84
13 111)
MALÉV Air Tours, Roosevelt tér
2, Budapest V (tel: 1186-614)
OTP Penta Tours, Váci utca
19–21, Budapest V
(tel: 1188-692)

## LANGUAGE

Hungarian (Magyar) lies outside the mainstream of European languages. Like Finnish, Estonian and Siberian Chuvash, it belongs to the Finno-Ugric group, so there is little room for guesswork and improvisation. Fortunately, English is spoken at hotel reception desks etc, though German is much more widely understood. Restaurants generally provide menus in the major European languages but, if you are eating out in an *Étterem*, or drinking in an ordinary Hungarian bar, you will have to point or resort to the phrase book. Shopping is less of a problem, at least in the major department stores but if you don't feel confident stick to Váci utca. Try at least to learn the Hungarian words for please, thank you, good day. It is a courtesy that will be appreciated and may win you friends. Hungarian has at least one thing going for it: the pronunciation is very straightforward and each word without exception carries a slight accentuation on the first syllable.

### Pronunciation

**Vowels**

*a* like English o in not
*á* like the a in car
*e* as in yes
*é* like day
*i* as in hit
*í* as in see
*o* like over
*ó* as above but longer
*ö* like the ur in fur
*ő* as above but longer
*u* like pull
*ú* as in rule
*ü* like the French *un* or German *fünf*
*ű* as above but longer

**Consonants**

*b, d, f, h, m, n, v, x, z* as in English
*c* like the ts in nets
*cs* like the ch in chap
*g* as in go
*gy* like the d in during
*j* like the y in yes
*ny* like ni in onion
*p* soft as in sip
*r* trilled like the Scottish
*s* like sh in ship
*sz* like s in so
*t* soft as in sit
*zs* like the s in pleasure

### The Basics

**Good day** Jó napot kivánok
**Yes** Igen
**No** Nem
**Please** Kérem
**Thank you** Köszönöm
**OK** Jó
**Excuse me** Bocsánat
**I'm English/American** Anglo-amerikai vagyok

| | |
|---|---|
| Monday | Hétfő |
| Tuesday | Kedd |
| Wednesday | Péntek |
| Thursday | Szombat |
| Friday | Vasárnap |
| Saturday | Szerda |
| Sunday | Csütörtök |
| One | Egy |
| Two | Két |
| Three | Három |
| Four | Négy |
| Five | Öt |
| Six | Hat |
| Seven | Hét |
| Eight | Nyolc |
| Nine | Kilenc |

| | |
|---|---|
| **Ten** | Tíz |
| **Eleven** | Tizenegy |
| **Twelve** | Tizenket |
| **Thirteen** | Tizenhárom |
| **Twenty** | Húsz |
| **Twenty-one** | Huszonegy |
| **Thirty** | Harminc |
| **Forty** | Negyven |
| **Fifty** | Ötven |
| **Sixty** | Hatvan |
| **Seventy** | Hetven |
| **Eighty** | Nyolcvan |
| **Ninety** | Kilencven |
| **One hundred** | Száz |

### Signs

| | |
|---|---|
| **Entrance** | Bejárat |
| **Exit** | Kijárat |
| **Arrival** | Érkezés |

*The language is difficult for most visitors, but music can easily be enjoyed without it. Classical concerts are held at the Vigado*

| | |
|---|---|
| **Departure** | Indulas |
| **Open** | Nyitva |
| **Closed** | Zárva |
| **Free admission** | a belépés ingyenes |
| **Toilet** | Mosdó or WC (pronounced vai-tsai) |
| **Men** | Férfi |
| **Women** | Női |
| **Hotel** | Szálló or Szálloda |
| **Room to let** | Szoba kiadó |
| **No smoking** | Tilos a dohányzás |
| **Caution** | Vigyázat |
| **Bus or train stop** | Megálló |
| **Tram** | Villamos |
| **Police station** | Rendőrség |
| **Airport** | Repülőtér |

### Other Useful Phrases

| | |
|---|---|
| **I'd like** | Szeretnék |
| **Where is/are?** | Hol van/vannak? |
| **How much is it?** | Mennyibe kerül? |
| **The bill please** | Kérem a számlát |

# INDEX

# INDEX

# INDEX

The Automobile Association would like to thank the following photographers and libraries for their assistance in the preparation of this book.

ERIC MEACHER took all the photographs in this book (© AA Photo Library) except:

MARY EVANS PICTURE LIBRARY 6/7 Peasants in battle array, 7 Admiral Horthy

NATURE PHOTOGRAPHERS LTD 79 Red-breasted flycatcher (R Tidman), 81 White stork (P R Sterry), 82 Grt Bustard (K J Carlson).